Eyewitness
INVENTION

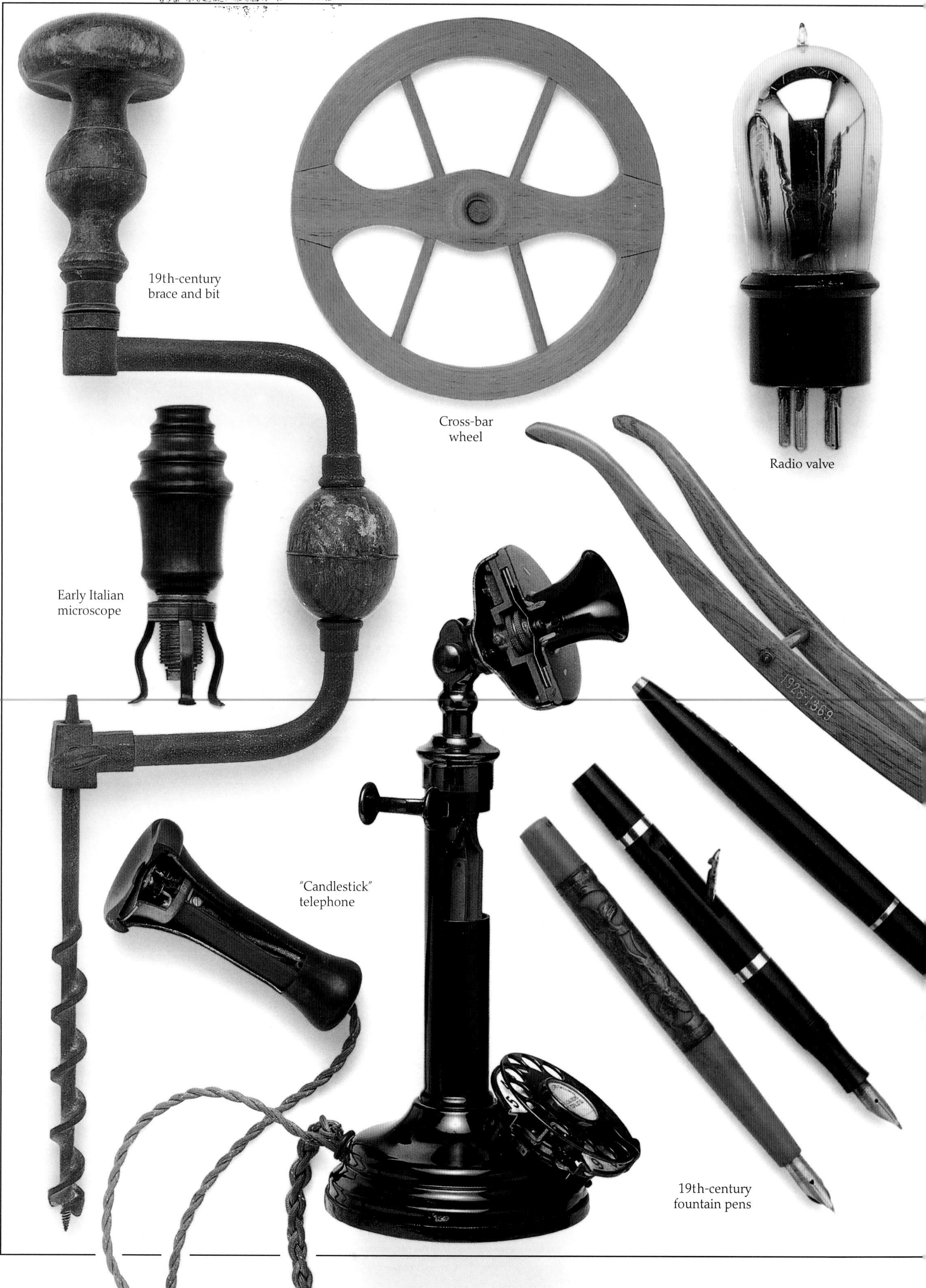

19th-century
brace and bit

Cross-bar
wheel

Radio valve

Early Italian
microscope

"Candlestick"
telephone

19th-century
fountain pens

Lenses from
daguerreotype camera

Ancient
Egyptian weights

Eyewitness
INVENTION

Written by
LIONEL BENDER

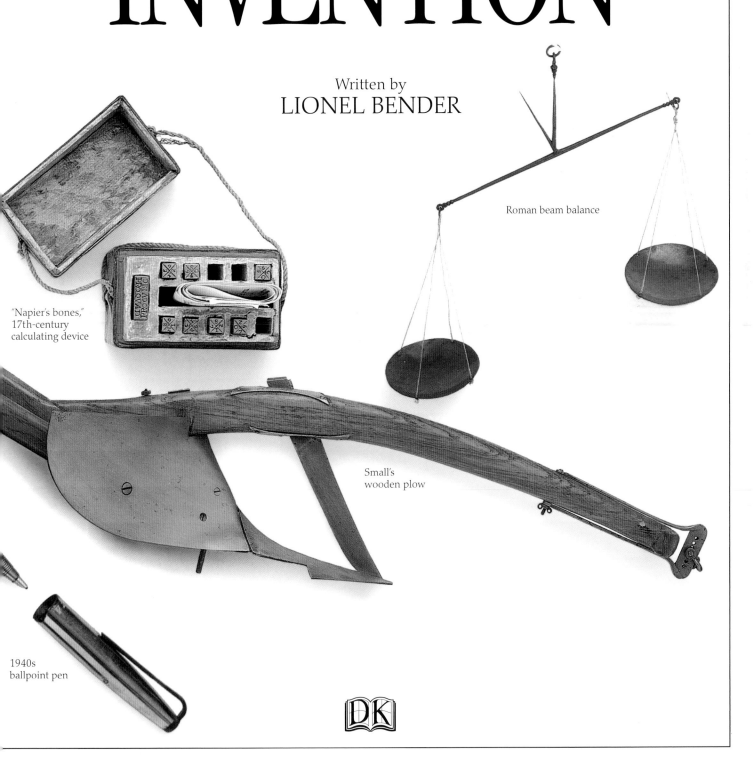

Roman beam balance

"Napier's bones,"
17th-century
calculating device

Small's
wooden plow

1940s
ballpoint pen

DK

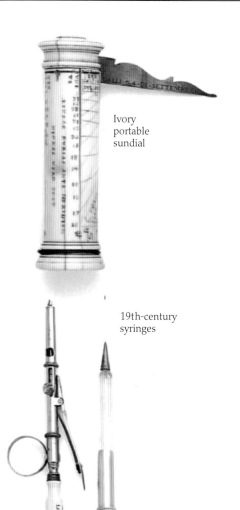

Ivory
portable
sundial

19th-century
syringes

Early
telephone
handset

LONDON, NEW YORK,
MELBOURNE, MUNICH, AND DELHI

Project editor Phil Wilkinson
Design Matthewson Bull
Senior editor Helen Parker
Senior art editors Jacquie Gulliver, Julia Harris
Production Louise Barratt
Picture research Kathy Lockley
Special photography Dave King
Additional text Peter Lafferty
Editorial consultants Staff of the Science Museum, London

Managing editors Linda Esposito, Andrew Macintyre
Managing art editor Jane Thomas
Category publisher Linda Martin
Art director Simon Webb
Editor and reference compiler Clare Hibbert
Art editor Joanna Pocock
Consultant Roger Bridgman
Production Jenny Jacoby
Picture research Celia Dearing
DTP designer Siu Yin Ho

REVISED EDITION
Consultant Chris Woodford

DK INDIA
Project editor Shatarupa Chaudhuri
Project art editor Nishesh Batnagar
Assistant editor Priyanka Kharbanda
Assistant art editor Honlung Zach Ragui
DTP designer Tarun Sharma
Picture researcher Sumedha Chopra

DK UK
Senior editor Caroline Stamps
Senior art editor Rachael Grady
Pre-production producers Adam Stoneham and Rachel Ng
Publisher Andrew Macintyre

DK US
US editor Margaret Parrish
Editorial director Nancy Ellwood

First American Edition, 1991
This American Edition, 2013
Published in the United States by
DK Publishing
345 Hudson Street, New York, New York 10014

13 14 15 16 17 10 9 8 7 6 5 4 3 2 1
001—187807—July/13
Copyright © 1991, © 2000, © 2013 Dorling Kindersley Limited
All rights reserved

A catalog record for this book is available from the Library of Congress.

ISBN: 978-1-4654-0901-0

ISBN: 978-1-4654-0902-7 (Library binding)

DK books are available at special discounts when purchased in bulk for sales
promotions, premiums, fundraising, or educational use. For details, contact:
DK Publishing Special Markets, 345 Hudson Street, New York, New York 10014
SpecialSales@dk.com

Color reproduction by Colourscan, Singapore
Printed and bound in China by South China Printing Co. Ltd

Discover more at
www.dk.com

Chinese
measuring
calipers

Ashanti
gold weights

Stone-headed ax
from Australia

Contents

Chinese mariner's compass

18th-century English compass

What is an invention?

A̲N INVENTION is something that was devised by human effort and that did not exist before. A discovery, on the other hand, is something that existed but was not yet known. Inventions rarely appear out of the blue. They usually result from the bringing together of existing technologies in a new and unique way. This can happen in response to some specific human need, or as a result of the inventor's desire to do something more quickly or efficiently, or even by accident. An invention can be the result of an individual's work, but is just as likely to come from the work of a team. Similar inventions have often appeared independently of each other at around the same time in different parts of the world.

Short handle

Pivot

Arms allow user to adjust depth and direction of cut

Long blade

Glass beads

Handle

FOOD FOR THOUGHT
The first tin cans had to be opened with a hammer and chisel. In 1855, British inventor Robert Yeates developed this claw-type can opener. The blade cut around the rim of the can using a levering action of the handle. Openers were given away with corned beef, called "bully" beef in the UK; the bull's head design was introduced around 1865.

GLASS
No one knows when the process of glassmaking (heating together soda and sand) was first discovered, although the Egyptians were making glazed beads in c. 4000 BCE. In the 1st century BCE, the Syrians probably introduced glassblowing, producing objects of many different shapes.

CUTTING EDGE
Scissors were invented more than 3,000 years ago, at about the same time in various places. Early types resemble tongs with a spring to push the blades apart. Like a seesaw, the scissors use the principle of the lever to increase cutting power.

Lid

Bull's head

Blade

IN THE CAN
The technique of heating food to a high temperature to kill harmful bacteria, then sealing it in airtight containers so that it can be stored for long periods was first perfected by Nicolas Appert in France in 1810. Appert used glass jars sealed with cork, but in 1811 two Englishmen, Bryan Donkin and John Hall, introduced the use of tin vacuum cans and set up the first food-canning factory.

Lock mechanism

Iron key

ZIP IT
The zipper was invented by American engineer Whitcomb Judson in 1893. It consisted of rows of hooks and eyes that were locked together by pulling a slide. The modern version, with interlocking metal teeth and slide, was developed from this by Gideon Sundback and patented in 1914.

LOCKED UP
In the earliest known locks the key was used to raise pins or tumblers so that a bolt could be moved. The two most common present-day types are the mortise and the Yale.

FIRE LIGHTERS
Modern matches were invented by British chemist John Walker in 1826. He used splinters of wood tipped with a mixture of chemicals that was ignited by heat generated by the friction of rubbing the tip on sandpaper. Matches like this were later known as lucifers, from the Latin for "light bearer."

R. BELL'S
IMPROVED
LUCIFERS

Sandpaper

Bulb from which air is extracted

PENCIL-IN THE DETAILS
Pencil "lead" was invented independently in France and Austria in the 1790s. Pencil makers soon discovered that by varying the relative amounts of the two main components of the lead (graphite and clay) they could make leads of different hardnesses.

Winder to take up tape into container

MASHED UP _below_
Paper was first produced in China around 100 CE. The earliest examples were made from a mixture of cloth, wood, and straw (p. 19).

LET THERE BE LIGHT _left_
The electric light bulb evolved from early experiments that showed that an electric current flowing through a wire creates heat due to resistance in the wire. If the current is strong enough, the wire glows white-hot. There were several independent inventors, including Thomas Edison and Joseph Swan. Carbon-filament lamps were mass-produced from the early 1880s.

Paper scroll

Circuit connector

MADE TO MEASURE _above_
The tape measure evolved from the measuring chains and rods first used by the Egyptians and then the Greeks and Romans. This example incorporates a notebook and dates from 1846.

Linen tape

Coulter to cut loose the soil

Moldboard to lift and turn soil

Plowshare

IN THE SOIL
The plow developed in about 5000 BCE from simple hoes and digging sticks that had been used by farmers for thousands of years. By changing the shape and size of its various parts it was gradually found that the soil could be cut, loosened, and turned in one operation.

Harness link to attach team of horses or oxen

A plowshare is the cutting edge of a moldboard of any plow

The story of an invention

THE CREATION OF AN INVENTION often involves many people, and inventions can take a long time to reach their final form. Sometimes an invention can take centuries to evolve, as the effects of different developments and new technologies are absorbed. By tracing the history of drilling tools, it is apparent that the invention of the familiar hand drill and bit evolved from refinements to the simple awl and the bow drill over hundreds of years. Among the earliest tools for boring holes were those used by the ancient Egyptians around 3000 BCE. Around 230 BCE, the Greek scientist Archimedes explored the use of levers and gears to transmit and increase forces. But it was not until the Middle Ages that the brace was developed for extra leverage; the wheel brace drill, which uses gears, evolved even more recently.

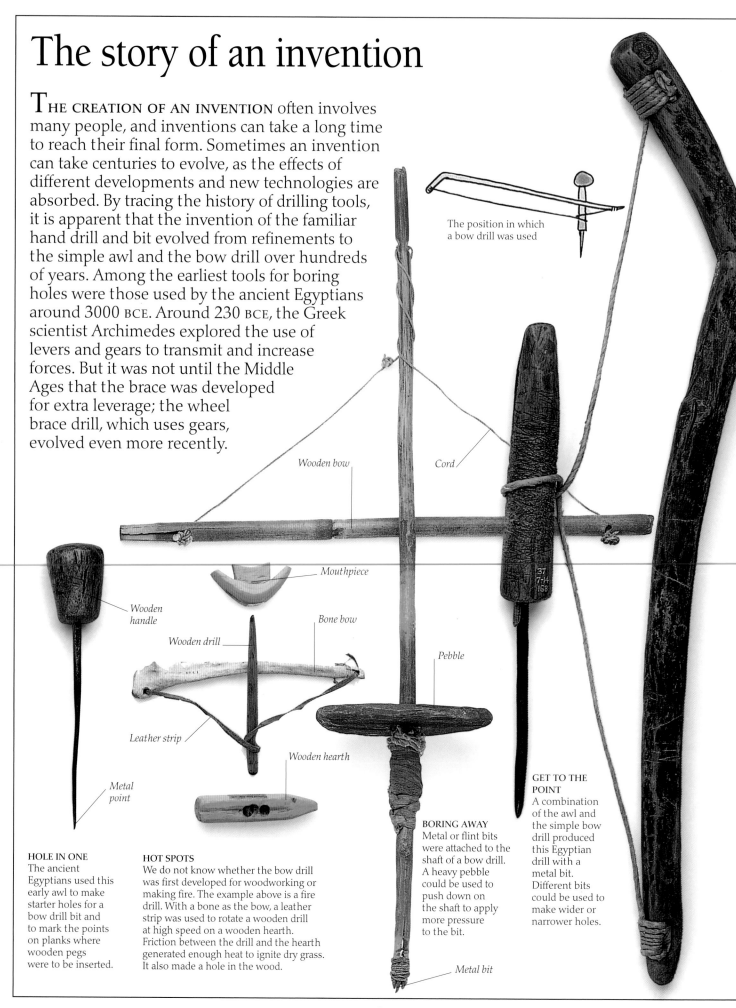

The position in which a bow drill was used

Wooden bow

Cord

Mouthpiece

Wooden handle

Bone bow

Wooden drill

Pebble

Leather strip

Wooden hearth

Metal point

GET TO THE POINT
A combination of the awl and the simple bow drill produced this Egyptian drill with a metal bit. Different bits could be used to make wider or narrower holes.

HOLE IN ONE
The ancient Egyptians used this early awl to make starter holes for a bow drill bit and to mark the points on planks where wooden pegs were to be inserted.

HOT SPOTS
We do not know whether the bow drill was first developed for woodworking or making fire. The example above is a fire drill. With a bone as the bow, a leather strip was used to rotate a wooden drill at high speed on a wooden hearth. Friction between the drill and the hearth generated enough heat to ignite dry grass. It also made a hole in the wood.

BORING AWAY
Metal or flint bits were attached to the shaft of a bow drill. A heavy pebble could be used to push down on the shaft to apply more pressure to the bit.

Metal bit

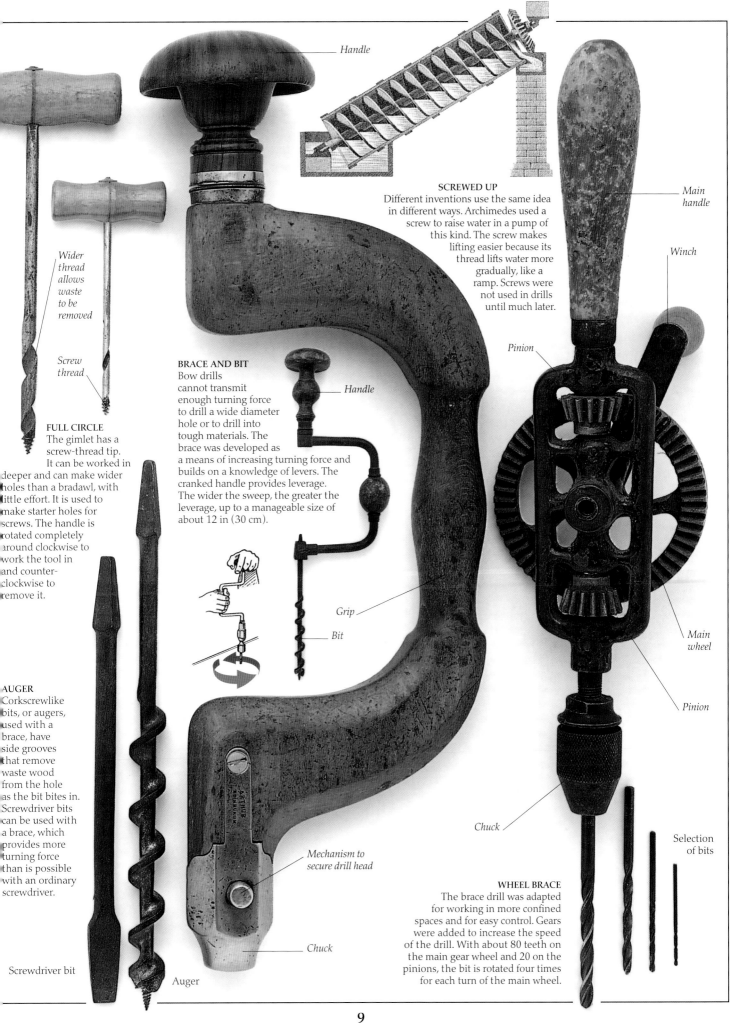

Handle

SCREWED UP
Different inventions use the same idea
in different ways. Archimedes used a
screw to raise water in a pump of
this kind. The screw makes
lifting easier because its
thread lifts water more
gradually, like a
ramp. Screws were
not used in drills
until much later.

*Main
handle*

Winch

*Wider
thread
allows
waste
to be
removed*

*Screw
thread*

BRACE AND BIT
Bow drills
cannot transmit
enough turning force
to drill a wide diameter
hole or to drill into
tough materials. The
brace was developed as
a means of increasing turning force and
builds on a knowledge of levers. The
cranked handle provides leverage.
The wider the sweep, the greater the
leverage, up to a manageable size of
about 12 in (30 cm).

Handle

Pinion

FULL CIRCLE
The gimlet has a
screw-thread tip.
It can be worked in
deeper and can make wider
holes than a bradawl, with
little effort. It is used to
make starter holes for
screws. The handle is
rotated completely
around clockwise to
work the tool in
and counter-
clockwise to
remove it.

*Main
wheel*

Grip

Bit

Pinion

AUGER
Corkscrewlike
bits, or augers,
used with a
brace, have
side grooves
that remove
waste wood
from the hole
as the bit bites in.
Screwdriver bits
can be used with
a brace, which
provides more
turning force
than is possible
with an ordinary
screwdriver.

Chuck

*Selection
of bits*

*Mechanism to
secure drill head*

WHEEL BRACE
The brace drill was adapted
for working in more confined
spaces and for easy control. Gears
were added to increase the speed
of the drill. With about 80 teeth on
the main gear wheel and 20 on the
pinions, the bit is rotated four times
for each turn of the main wheel.

Screwdriver bit

Auger

Chuck

Tools

ABOUT 3.75 MILLION YEARS AGO, our distant ancestors evolved an upright stance and began to live on open grassland. With their hands free for new uses, they scavenged abandoned carcasses and gathered plant food. Gradually, early people developed the use of tools. They used pebbles and stones to cut meat and to smash open bones for marrow. Later they chipped away at the edges of their stones so that they could cut better. Nearly two million years ago, flint was being shaped into axes and arrowheads, and bones were used as clubs and hammers. About 1.4 million years ago, humankind discovered fire. Now able to cook food, our recent ancestors created a varied toolkit for hunting wild animals. When they started to farm, a different set of tools was needed.

Stone blade

DUAL-PURPOSE IMPLEMENT
The adze was a development of the ax that appeared in the 8th millennium BCE. Its blade was set almost at right angles to the handle. This North Papuan tool could be used either as an ax (as here) or an adze by changing the position of the blade.

Split wooden handle

STICKY END
This ax from Australia represents the next stage of development from the hand ax. A stone was set in gum in the bend of a flexible strip of wood, and the two halves of the piece of wood were bound together. The ax was probably used to kill wild animals.

AN EARLY FLINT TOOL
This flint handax, found in Kent, England, was first roughly shaped with a stone hammer (above) then refined with a bone one. It is perhaps 20,000 years old. It dates from a period known as the Old Stone Age, or Paleolithic period, when flint was the main material used to make tools.

Socket to take shaft

Hole for binding cord

NEXT BEST THING
Where flint was not available, softer stones were used for tools, as with this rough-stone axhead. Not all stones could be made as sharp as flint.

AX TO GRIND
To make this axhead, a lump of stone was probably rubbed against rocks and ground with pebbles until it was smooth and polished.

BRONZE TOOLS
The use of bronze for making tools and weapons began in Asia about 5,000 years ago. In Europe, the Bronze Age lasted from about 2000 to 500 BCE.

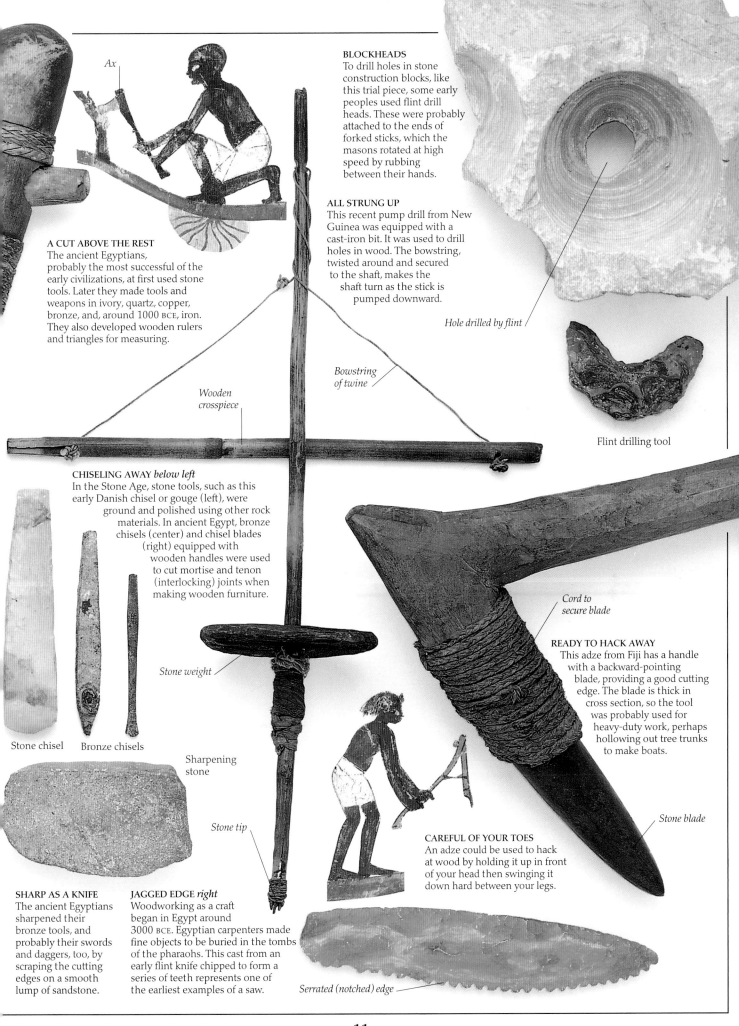

Ax

A CUT ABOVE THE REST
The ancient Egyptians,
probably the most successful of the
early civilizations, at first used stone
tools. Later they made tools and
weapons in ivory, quartz, copper,
bronze, and, around 1000 BCE, iron.
They also developed wooden rulers
and triangles for measuring.

BLOCKHEADS
To drill holes in stone
construction blocks, like
this trial piece, some early
peoples used flint drill
heads. These were probably
attached to the ends of
forked sticks, which the
masons rotated at high
speed by rubbing
between their hands.

ALL STRUNG UP
This recent pump drill from New
Guinea was equipped with a
cast-iron bit. It was used to drill
holes in wood. The bowstring,
twisted around and secured
to the shaft, makes the
shaft turn as the stick is
pumped downward.

Hole drilled by flint

*Bowstring
of twine*

*Wooden
crosspiece*

Flint drilling tool

CHISELING AWAY *below left*
In the Stone Age, stone tools, such as this
early Danish chisel or gouge (left), were
ground and polished using other rock
materials. In ancient Egypt, bronze
chisels (center) and chisel blades
(right) equipped with
wooden handles were used
to cut mortise and tenon
(interlocking) joints when
making wooden furniture.

Stone weight

*Cord to
secure blade*

READY TO HACK AWAY
This adze from Fiji has a handle
with a backward-pointing
blade, providing a good cutting
edge. The blade is thick in
cross section, so the tool
was probably used for
heavy-duty work, perhaps
hollowing out tree trunks
to make boats.

Stone chisel   Bronze chisels

*Sharpening
stone*

Stone tip

Stone blade

CAREFUL OF YOUR TOES
An adze could be used to hack
at wood by holding it up in front
of your head then swinging it
down hard between your legs.

SHARP AS A KNIFE
The ancient Egyptians
sharpened their
bronze tools, and
probably their swords
and daggers, too, by
scraping the cutting
edges on a smooth
lump of sandstone.

JAGGED EDGE *right*
Woodworking as a craft
began in Egypt around
3000 BCE. Egyptian carpenters made
fine objects to be buried in the tombs
of the pharaohs. This cast from an
early flint knife chipped to form a
series of teeth represents one of
the earliest examples of a saw.

Serrated (notched) edge

The wheel

THE WHEEL is probably the most important mechanical invention of all time. Wheels are found in most machines, in clocks, windmills, and steam engines, as well as in vehicles such as the automobile and the bicycle. The wheel probably appeared in Mesopotamia, part of modern Iraq, at least 5,000 years ago, and was first used by potters to help work their clay. Later, wheels were fitted to carts, transforming transportation and making it possible to move heavy materials and bulky objects with relative ease. These early wheels were solid, cut from sections of wooden planks, which were fastened together. Spoked wheels appeared later, from around 2000 BCE. They were lighter and were used for chariots. Bearings, which enabled the wheel to turn more easily, were introduced around 100 BCE.

POTTER'S WHEEL
By 300 BCE the Greeks and Egyptians had invented the kick wheel. The disk's heavy weight enabled it to turn at near constant speed.

Tripartite wheel

Seat

Protective shield for driver

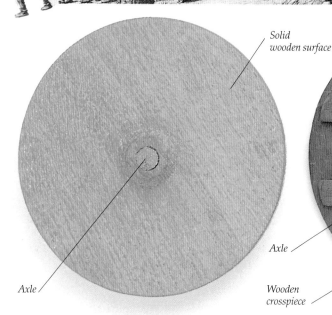

STONE-AGE BUILDERS *left*
Before the wheel, rollers made from tree trunks were probably used to push objects such as huge building stones into place. The tree trunks had the same effect as wheels, but a lot of effort was needed to put the rollers in place and keep the load balanced.

Peg to hold wheel in place

Solid wooden surface

Axle

Axle

Axle

Wooden crosspiece

Axle

SCARCE BUT SOLID
Early wheels were sometimes solid disks of wood cut from tree trunks. These were not common because the wheel originated in places where trees were scarce. Solid wooden chariot wheels have been found in Denmark.

PLANK WHEEL
Three-part (or "tripartite") wheels were made of planks fastened together by wooden or metal crosspieces. One of the earliest forms of wheel, they are still used in some countries because they are suitable for bad roads.

ROLLING STONE
In some places, where wood was scarce, stone was used for wheels instead. It was heavy, but long-lasting. The stone wheel originated in China and Turkey.

WHEELS AT WAR
The wheel made possible the chariot, which originated in Mesopotamia around 2000 BCE.

Leather thongs

Wooden chassis beam

CROSSBAR
The horse was strapped to the crossbar, which was bound to the chassis with leather thongs.

Peg to hold wheel in place

Chassis

Fixed axle

FIXED IN PLACE
The fixed axle was rigid. It was attached to the chassis of the vehicle. The wheel turned around the axle.

Wheel

LEATHER BEARING
Around 100 BCE, the Celts of France and Germany made carts with simple axle bearings. These consisted of leather sleeves that fit between the axle and the wheel hub. They reduced friction, allowing the wheel to turn easily.

Leather axle bearing

HARVEST HOME
Wheels like this, with metal rims to lessen wear, were made as early as 2000 BCE. They were used throughout the Middle Ages.

Chassis

Rotating axle

MOVING AXLE
The moving axle was fixed rigidly to the wheel and turned with the wheel.

Wheel

Early Middle Eastern cart

Roller bearings

ROLLERS
Around 100 BCE, Danish wagon-makers may have tried putting wooden rollers around the axle in an attempt to make the wheel turn more smoothly.

Roller bearings

Holes make wheel lighter.

Cut stone construction

Axle

EARLY SEMISOLID WHEEL
Wheels could be made lighter by cutting out sections of wood. Wheels of this type were made in the centuries around 2000 BCE.

Crossbar

Axle

Spokes to strengthen wheel

CROSSBAR WHEEL
If large sections of a wheel were cut away, the wheel could be strengthened with struts or crossbars. From here it was a small step to the spoked wheel.

Metalworking

GOLD AND SILVER occur naturally in their metallic state. From early times, people found lumps of these metals and used them for simple ornaments. But the first useful metal to be worked was copper, which had to be extracted from rocks, or ores, by heating on a fierce fire. The next step was to make bronze. This is an alloy—a metal made by mixing two metallic elements together. Bronze, an alloy of copper and tin, was strong and did not rust or decay. It was easy to work by melting and pouring into a shaped mold in a process called casting. Because bronze is strong and easy to work, everything from swords to jewelry was made of it. Iron was first used around 2000 BCE. Iron ores were burned with charcoal, producing an impure form of the metal. Iron was plentiful, but difficult to melt. At first it had to be worked by hammering rather than casting.

Roman iron nails, about 88 CE

CASTING—FINAL STAGE
When cold, the mold was broken open and the object removed. Solid bronze is far harder than copper and can be hammered to give a sharp cutting edge. Because of this, bronze became the first metal to be widely used.

Bloom of iron

Iron ore

Partially hammered bloom

BLOOM OF IRON
Early furnaces were not hot enough to melt iron and so the metal was produced as a spongy lump, called a bloom. The bloom was hammered into shape while red-hot.

CASTING—FIRST STAGE
The first stage in producing bronze was to heat copper and tin ores in a large bowl on a simple furnace. Bronze is easier to melt and separate than copper alone.

CASTING—SECOND STAGE
The molten bronze was poured into a mold and allowed to cool and solidify. This process is called casting. Knowledge of bronze casting had reached Europe by about 3500 BCE and China several centuries later.

IRON SWORD-MAKING
In the first century CE, iron swords were made by twisting and hammering together several strips or rods of iron. This process was called pattern welding.

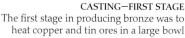

PINS AND NEEDLES
Bronze could be worked into delicate, small objects, such as pins and needles. It was also used for large objects, such as bells and statues.

ROMAN NAILS
These iron nails were removed from Roman sites in London and Scotland.

IN A BLAST FURNACE
Cast iron, made by pouring molten iron into a mold, had to wait for the invention of the blast furnace in China in the 5th century BCE. The blast furnace was invented in the West in the 14th century CE.

An early form of horseshoe, a horse hobble was made of wrought iron. It was strapped in place over the hoof

Hoop to accept strap

Flat surface to take base of horse's foot

AFRICAN IRON
Iron making in simple furnaces could still be found in parts of Africa in the 1930s. These items made in the Sudan were produced in a clay furnace and hammered into shape.

Quer—a type of hoe made of wrought iron

GETTING THE POINT
Iron was often used for weapons, which could be quite elaborate. This spearhead had a wooden handle.

Barbed point

BRONZE ORNAMENTS
Bronze bracelets were often decorated with fine patterns. Ornamental hairpins sometimes had large hollow heads, covered with patterns.

Bracelet

Hairpin

IRON HAMMER *right*
Iron has been used for making hammers for centuries. This simple iron hammer comes from the Sudan and dates from about 1930.

Iron strands bound together for strength

Point made of pieces of iron hammered together

DECORATIVE SWORDS
Pattern welding produced a strong blade that could be sharpened and had a fine, strong cutting edge. The twisted iron strips forming the blade produced an ornamental pattern along its length.

Finished sword

SMALL HANDS?
Bronze swords often had ornamental handles and finger guards. The handles were usually very short and could not be held comfortably by hands as large as ours.

Weights and measures

THE FIRST SYSTEMS of weights and measures were developed in ancient Egypt and Babylon. They were needed to weigh crops, measure plots of farmland, and standardize commercial transactions. Around 3500 BCE the Egyptians were using scales. They had standard weights and a measurement of length called the royal cubit, equal to about 21 in (52 cm). The Code of Hammurabi, a document recording the laws of the king of Babylon from 1792 to 1750 BCE, refers to standard weights and different units of weight and length. By Greek and Roman times, scales, balances, and rulers were in everyday use. Present-day systems of weights and measures—the imperial (foot, pound) and metric (meter, gram)—were established in the 1300s and 1790s, respectively.

Early Egyptian stone weights

Egyptian metal weights

HEAVY METAL
Early Egyptians used rocks as standard weights, but around 2000 BCE, as metalworking developed, weights cast in bronze and iron were used.

Hook for object to be weighed

WORTH THEIR WEIGHT IN GOLD
The Ashanti, Africans from a gold-mining region of modern Ghana, rose to power in the 18th century. They made standard weights in the form of gold ornaments.

Fish

Scorpion

Sword

Pointer

WEIGHING HIM
This ancient Egyptian balance is being used in a ceremony called "Weighing the heart," which was supposed to take place after a person's death.

OFF BALANCE
This Roman beam balance for weighing coins consists of a bronze rod pivoted at the center. Objects to be weighed were placed on a pan hung from one end of the beam and were balanced against known weights hung from the other end. A pointer at the center of the beam showed when the pans balanced.

Pan

Hollow to take smaller weights

NESTING WEIGHTS
With simple balances, sets of standard weights are used. Large or small weights are put on or taken off until the balance is horizontal. These are French 17th-century nesting weights, one fitting neatly into another to make a neat stack.

Scale in inches and centimeters

USING THE STEELYARD *right*
On a steelyard, the weight is moved along the long arm, and the distance from the pivot to the balance-point, read off the scale, gives the object's weight. For traveling merchants, its advantage was that they did not need to carry a large range of weights.

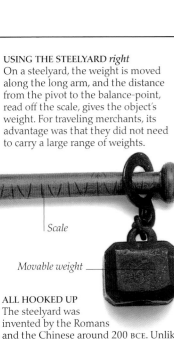

Scale

Movable weight

ALL HOOKED UP
The steelyard was invented by the Romans and the Chinese around 200 BCE. Unlike a simple balance, it had one arm longer than the other. A sack of grain, for example, would be hung from the short arm and a single weight moved along the long arm until it balanced. This example dates from the 17th century.

A BIG STEP *above right*
This British size stick for measuring people's feet starts with size 1 as a 4⅓ inch length and increases in stages of one-third of an inch (a measurement called a barleycorn).

FILLED TO THE BRIM *below*
Liquids must be placed in a container, such as this copper pitcher used by a distiller, to be measured. The volume mark is in the narrow part of the neck, so the right measure can be seen instantly.

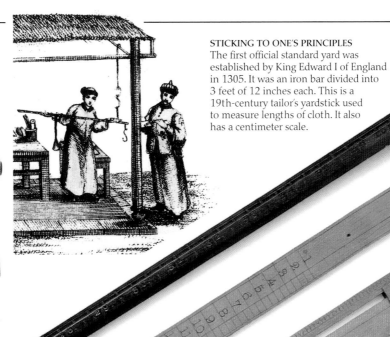

STICKING TO ONE'S PRINCIPLES
The first official standard yard was established by King Edward I of England in 1305. It was an iron bar divided into 3 feet of 12 inches each. This is a 19th-century tailor's yardstick used to measure lengths of cloth. It also has a centimeter scale.

Foot positioned here

Adjustable jaw

GRIPPED TIGHTLY *above right*
Wrenchlike sliding calipers, used to measure the width of solid objects such as stone, metal, and wooden building components, were invented at least 2,000 years ago. Measurements are read off a scale on a fixed arm, as on this replica of a caliper from China.

FLEXIBLE FRIEND *left*
Tape measures are used in situations where a ruler is too rigid. Measuring people for clothes is one of the most familiar uses of the tape measure, but much longer tapes are also used.

GETTING IT RIGHT
One of the most important things about weights and measures is that they should be standardized so that each unit is always of identical value. These men are testing weights and measures to ensure that they are accurate.

Volume mark here

NO SHORT MEASURES
This Indian grain measure was used to dispense standard quantities of loose items. A store owner would sell the grain by the measureful rather than weighing different quantities each time.

17

Pen and ink

WRITTEN RECORDS first became necessary following the development of agriculture in a Middle Eastern region known as the Fertile Crescent about 10,000 years ago. The Babylonians and ancient Egyptians inscribed stones, bones, and clay tablets with symbols and simple pictures to keep records of land tenure, irrigation rights, and harvests and to write down tax assessments and accounts. As writing implements they first used flints, then the whittled ends of sticks. Around 2500 BCE the Chinese and Egyptians developed inks made from lampblack, obtained from the soot and oil burned in lamps, mixed with water and plant gums. They could make different colored inks from earth pigments such as red ocher. Oil-based inks were developed in the Middle Ages for use in printing (pp. 26–27), but writing inks and lead pencils are modern inventions. More recent developments, such as the fountain pen and the ballpoint pen, were designed to get the ink on the paper without having to refill the pen.

LIGHT AS A FEATHER
A quill—the hollow shaft of a feather—was first used as a pen around 500 CE. Dried and cleaned goose, swan, or turkey feathers were most popular because the thick shaft held the ink and the pen was easy to handle. The tip was shaved to a point with a knife and split slightly to ensure that the ink flowed smoothly.

HEAVY READING
The first writing that we have evidence of is on Mesopotamian clay tablets. A scribe used a wedge-shaped stylus to make marks in the clay while it was wet. The clay dried to leave a permanent record. The marks that make up this kind of writing are called cuneiform, meaning wedge-shaped.

A PRESSING POINT
In the 1st millennium BCE the Egyptians wrote with reeds and rushes, which they cut to form a point. They used the reed pens to apply lampblack to papyrus.

Chinese characters

ON PAPYRUS

Ancient Egyptian and Assyrian scribes wrote on papyrus. This was made from pith taken from the stem of the papyrus plant. The pith was removed, arranged in layers, and hammered to make a sheet. The Assyrian scribe (left) is recording a battle. The papyrus (right) is from ancient Egypt.

STROKE OF GENIUS
The ancient Chinese wrote their characters in ink using brushes of camels' or rats' hairs. Clusters of hairs were glued and bound to the end of a stick. For fine work on silk they used brushes made of just a few hairs glued into the end of a hollow reed.

Ink reservoir for early ballpoint

Fiber tip

SOFTLY DOES IT
Fiber or felt-tipped pens were invented in the 1960s. A stick of absorbent material acts as the ink reservoir. The tip-stalk, embedded in the reservoir, contains narrow channels through which ink flows as soon as the tip touches the paper.

Lever for filling pen

Free-moving ball

ON THE BALL
The ballpoint pen was developed by John Loud of the United States in the 1880s. The modern version was invented by J. László and Georg Bíró in the 1940s. At the tip of an ink-filled plastic tube is a tiny, free-moving metal ball. Ink flows from the tube through a narrow gap to the ball, which transfers the ink to the paper.

METAL NIBS
Dip pens, such as those formerly used in schools, had a wooden stem, metal nib holder, and changeable nibs. Early pen nibs, like these, were all steel. Present-day versions are often tipped with durable metals such as osmium or tungsten.

CLOGGING UP THE WORKS
Fountain pens were invented in Europe around 1800. Rubber tubing, inside a metal stem, was used to hold the ink, which was a solution of natural plant dyes such as indigo. Unless the dyestuff was finely ground, the ink would clog the nib. In 1884, Lewis E. Waterman invented the first real fountain pen.

FIT FOR A KING
The scribes of the Middle Ages used quill pens to produce their elaborately decorated manuscripts. This example records the coronation of King Henry of Castile in the l5th century. It shows the delicate strokes that were possible with very simple equipment.

Sharpened point

Range of nibs for dip pens

Papermaking
The earliest fragments of paper that have been discovered come from China and date from around 100 CE. Knowledge of papermaking eventually spread to Europe via the Islamic world. The basic process remained similar to that used in China. Paper was made from wood pulp and rags that were soaked in water and beaten into a pulp.

TRAY BY TRAY *right*
A tray with wire grids was lowered into the pulp, the grid removed, and surplus water drained.

HANGING OUT TO DRY
The resulting sheet was taken off the grid and put on a piece of felt before finally being hung to dry.

MISSED THE POINT
Quill pens were worn down by the constant scraping against the rough paper or parchment and from time to time had to be resharpened. In the 17th century, quill sharpeners were invented. The worn end of the quill was snipped off neatly.

Lighting

THE FIRST ARTIFICIAL LIGHT came from fire, but this was dangerous and difficult to carry around. Then, about 20,000 years ago, people realized that they could get light by burning oil, and the first lamps appeared. These were hollowed-out rocks full of animal fat. Lamps with wicks of vegetable fibers were first made in about 1000 BCE. Initially, they had a simple channel to hold the wick; later, the wick was held in a spout. Candles appeared about 5,000 years ago. A candle is just a wick surrounded by wax or tallow. When the wick is lit, the flame melts some of the wax or tallow, which burns to give off light. So a candle is really an oil lamp in a more convenient form. Oil lamps and candles were the chief source of artificial light until gas lighting became common in the 19th century; electric lighting took over in the early part of the 20th century.

CAVE LIGHT
When early people made fire for cooking and heating, they realized that it also gave off light. So the cooking fire provided the first source of artificial light. From this it was a simple step to make a brushwood torch so that light could be carried around or placed high in a dark cave.

Wick

COSTLY CANDLES
The first candles were made over 5,000 years ago. Wax or tallow was poured over a hanging wick and left to cool. Such candles were too expensive for most people.

Container for wax

Wick

SHELL-SHAPED *right*
By pouring oil in the body and laying a wick in the neck, a shell can be used as a lamp. This one is from the 19th century, but shell lamps appeared centuries earlier.

Spout for wick

UP THE SPOUT
Saucerlike pottery lamps have been made for thousands of years. They burned olive oil or oil from colza, the root of the rutabaga. This one was probably made in Egypt about 2,000 years ago.

COVERED OVER *right*
The Romans made clay lamps with a covered top to keep the oil clean. The lamps sometimes had more than one spout and wick to give more light.

Hole for wick

Wick

HOLLOWED OUT *left*
The most basic form of lamp is a hollowed-out stone. This one came from the Shetland Islands, Scotland, and was used during the 19th century. Similar examples have been found in the caves at Lascaux, France, dating from about 15,000 years ago.

MOLDS
Candles have been made in molds since the 15th century. They made candlemaking easier, but were not widely used until the process was mechanized in the 19th century.

LIGHTS OUT
Conical snuffers were often used to put out candles. There was no smell and little risk of being burned.

DRY AS TINDER
Before the introduction of matches, tinderboxes were used to light fires and lamps. A spark was made by striking a flint (the striker) against a piece of metal (the steel). Some dry material (the tinder) in the box would catch fire.

Handle

Steel

Tinder

Lid

Candle holder

Striker

Tinderbox

Cover to put out fire

TRIMMING THE WICK
With the appearance of more sophisticated oil lamps, elaborate tools were made to cut the wicks. This wick trimmer clips the wick and flicks the debris into the container.

CANDLE POWER *above*
One candle produces little light—one candle power, called one candela.

PROTECTOR
Lanterns were used to shield the flame from the wind and to reduce the risk of fire.

Handle to raise candle

SWEETNESS AND LIGHT
Another way to make a candle was to use wax collected from a beehive. This could be rolled into a cylinder shape.

ON THE STREETS
This engraving shows the first candle streetlight being lit in Paris in 1667. The lamplighter had to climb a stepladder to reach the lantern.

TWISTER
This candlestick has a spiral mechanism. The user twists the handle as the candle burns down to keep the flame at the same level.

Timekeeping

KEEPING TRACK OF TIME became important as soon as people began to cultivate the land. But it was the astronomers of ancient Egypt, some 3,000 years ago, who used the regular movement of the Sun through the sky to tell time more accurately. The Egyptian shadow clock was a sundial, indicating time by the position of a shadow falling across markers. Other early devices for telling time depended on the regular burning of a candle or the flow of water through a small hole. The first mechanical clocks used the regular rocking of a metal rod, called a foliot, to regulate the movement of a hand around a dial. Later clocks use pendulums, which swing back and forth. The escapement ensures that this regular movement is transmitted to the gears, which drive the hands.

BOOK OF HOURS
Medieval books of hours—prayer books with pictures of peasant life in the different months—show how important seasons were to people working on the land. This is the illustration for the month of March, from the *Très Riches Heures*, created for John, Duke of Berry, in France.

COUNTING HOURS
The ancient Egyptian *merkhet* was used to observe the movement of certain stars across the sky, allowing the hours of the night to be calculated. This one belonged to an astronomer-priest of about 600 BCE named Bes.

Holes to take pin

Folding gnomon

COLUMN DIAL
This small ivory sundial has two gnomons (pointers), one for summer and one for winter.

Cover

String gnomon

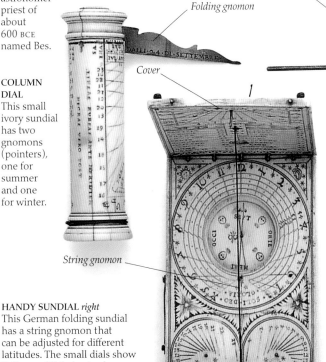

HANDY SUNDIAL *right*
This German folding sundial has a string gnomon that can be adjusted for different latitudes. The small dials show Italian and Babylonian hours. The dial also indicates the length of the day and the position of the Sun in the zodiac.

TIBETAN TIMESTICK
The Tibetan timestick relied on the shadow cast by a pin through an upright rod. The pin would be placed in different positions according to the time of the year.

WATER CLOCK
Su Sung's water clock, built in 1088, was housed in a tower 35 ft (10 m) high. Its water wheel paused after each bucket filled, marking intervals of time. Gears conveyed the motion to a globe.

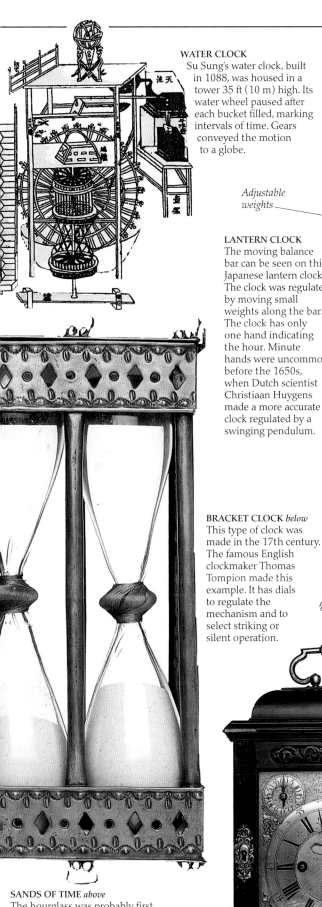

Adjustable weights

LANTERN CLOCK
The moving balance bar can be seen on this Japanese lantern clock. The clock was regulated by moving small weights along the bar. The clock has only one hand indicating the hour. Minute hands were uncommon before the 1650s, when Dutch scientist Christiaan Huygens made a more accurate clock regulated by a swinging pendulum.

CHRISTIAAN HUYGENS
This Dutch scientist made the first practical pendulum clock in the mid-17th century.

VERGE WATCH
Until the 16th century, clocks were powered by falling weights and could not be moved around. The use of a coiled spring to drive the hands meant that portable clocks and watches could be made, but they were not very accurate. This example dates from the 17th century.

BRACKET CLOCK *below*
This type of clock was made in the 17th century. The famous English clockmaker Thomas Tompion made this example. It has dials to regulate the mechanism and to select striking or silent operation.

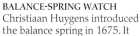

BALANCE-SPRING WATCH
Christiaan Huygens introduced the balance spring in 1675. It allowed much more accurate watch movements to be made. Thomas Tompion, the maker of this watch, introduced the balance spring to England, giving that country a leading position in watchmaking.

SANDS OF TIME *above*
The hourglass was probably first used in the Middle Ages, around 1300 CE, although this is a much later example. Sand flowed through a narrow hole between two glass bulbs. When all the sand was in the lower bulb, a fixed time had passed.

Harnessing power

Since the dawn of history, people have looked for sources of power to make work easier and more efficient. First they made human muscle power more effective with the use of machines such as cranes and treadmills. It was soon realized that the muscle power of animals such as horses, mules, and oxen was much greater than that of humans. Animals were trained to pull heavy loads and work in treadmills. Other useful sources of power came from wind and water. The first sailing ships were made in Egypt about 5,000 years ago. The Romans used water mills for grinding corn during the 1st century BCE. Water power remained important and is still widely used today. Windmills spread westward across Europe in the Middle Ages, when people began to look for a more efficient way of grinding corn.

MUSCLE POWER
Dogs are still used in Arctic regions to pull sleds, although elsewhere in the world horses, oxen, and other animals have been widely used as working animals. Horses were also used to turn machinery such as grindstones and pumps.

POST MILL
Many of the earliest windmills were post mills. The whole mill could turn around its central post to face into the wind. Made of lumber, many post mills were quite fragile and could blow over in a storm.

HAUL AWAY!
This 15th-century crane in Bruges, Belgium, was worked by men walking on a treadmill. It is shown lifting wine kegs. Other simple machines, such as the lever and pulley, were the mainstay of early industry. It is said that around 250 BCE the Greek scientist Archimedes could singlehandedly move a large ship using a system of pulleys. It is not known exactly how he did this.

Tail pole

THE FIRST WATER WHEELS
From around 70 BCE we have records of the Romans using two types of water wheel to grind corn. In the undershot wheel, the water passes beneath the wheel; in the overshot wheel, the water flows over the top. The latter can be three times more efficient because it gets extra power from the weight of the water falling on the blades.

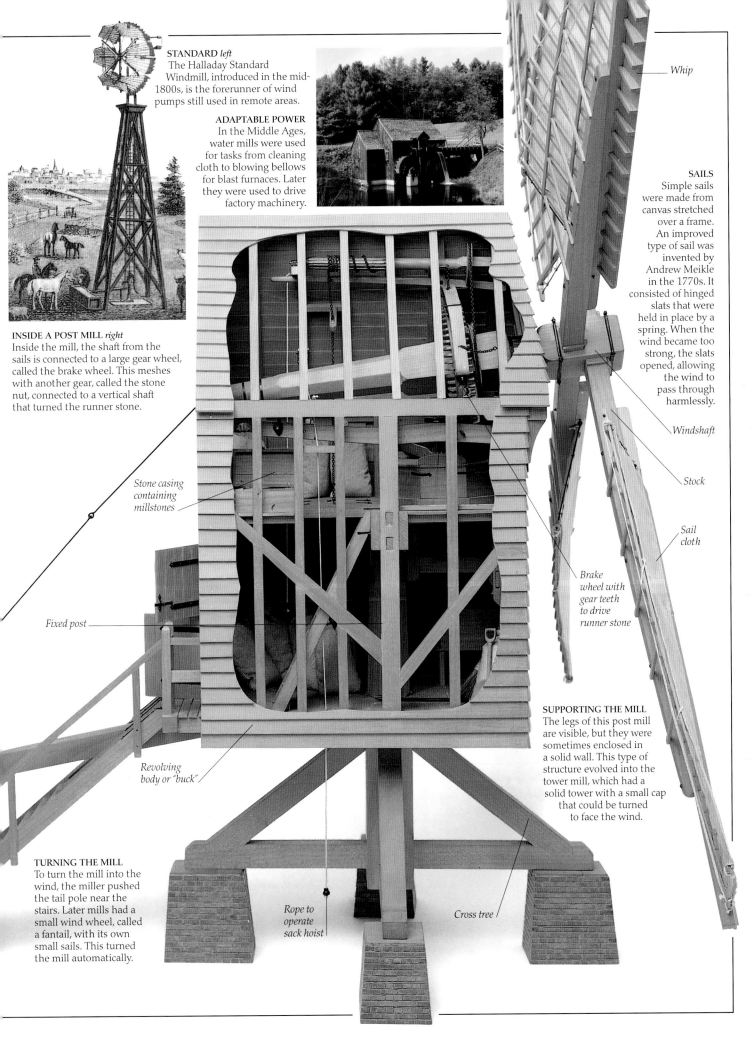

STANDARD *left*
The Halladay Standard Windmill, introduced in the mid-1800s, is the forerunner of wind pumps still used in remote areas.

ADAPTABLE POWER
In the Middle Ages, water mills were used for tasks from cleaning cloth to blowing bellows for blast furnaces. Later they were used to drive factory machinery.

Whip

SAILS
Simple sails were made from canvas stretched over a frame. An improved type of sail was invented by Andrew Meikle in the 1770s. It consisted of hinged slats that were held in place by a spring. When the wind became too strong, the slats opened, allowing the wind to pass through harmlessly.

INSIDE A POST MILL *right*
Inside the mill, the shaft from the sails is connected to a large gear wheel, called the brake wheel. This meshes with another gear, called the stone nut, connected to a vertical shaft that turned the runner stone.

Windshaft

Stone casing containing millstones

Stock

Sail cloth

Brake wheel with gear teeth to drive runner stone

Fixed post

SUPPORTING THE MILL
The legs of this post mill are visible, but they were sometimes enclosed in a solid wall. This type of structure evolved into the tower mill, which had a solid tower with a small cap that could be turned to face the wind.

Revolving body or "buck"

TURNING THE MILL
To turn the mill into the wind, the miller pushed the tail pole near the stairs. Later mills had a small wind wheel, called a fantail, with its own small sails. This turned the mill automatically.

Rope to operate sack hoist

Cross tree

Printing

BEFORE PRINTING BEGAN, each copy of every book had to be written out laboriously by hand. This made books rare and expensive. The first people to print books were the Chinese and Japanese in the 6th century. Characters and pictures were engraved on wooden, clay, or ivory blocks. When a paper sheet was pressed against the inked block, the characters were printed on the sheet by the raised areas of the engraving. This is known as letterpress printing. The greatest advance in printing was the invention of movable type—single letters on small individual blocks that could be set in lines and reused. This innovation also began in China in the 11th century. Movable type was first used in Europe in the 15th century. The most important pioneer was German goldsmith Johannes Gutenberg. He invented typecasting—a method of making large amounts of accurate movable type cheaply and quickly. After Gutenberg's work in the late 1430s, printing with movable type spread quickly across Europe.

This early Japanese wooden printing block has a complete passage of text carved into a single block of wood.

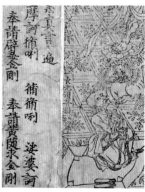

FROM THE EAST
This early Chinese book was printed with wooden blocks, each of which bore a single character.

EARLY TYPE
Blocks with one character were first used in China in about 1040. These are casts of early Turkish types.

PUNCHES
Gutenberg used a hard metal punch, carved with a letter. This was hammered into a soft metal to make a mold.

Letter stamped in metal

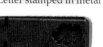

IN GOOD SHAPE
Each "matrix" bore the impression of a letter or symbol.

POURING HOT METAL
A ladle was used to pour molten metal, a mixture of tin, lead, and antimony, into the mold to form a piece of type.

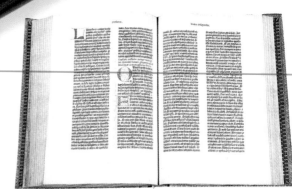

THE GUTENBERG BIBLE
In 1455, Gutenberg produced the first large printed book, a Bible that is still regarded as a masterpiece of the printer's art.

TYPE MOLD
The matrix was placed in the bottom of a mold like this. The mold was then closed and the molten metal was poured in through the top. The sides were opened to release the type.

Mold inserted here

Spring to hold mold closed

Screw to secure blade

Metal blade

CLOSE SHAVE
A type plane was used to shave the backs of the metal type to ensure that all the letters were exactly the same height.

Piece of type

How the traditional composing stick was held in the hand

REVERSED WORDS *above*
Early printers arranged type into words on a small tray called a composing stick. The letters have to be arranged upside down and from right to left, because the printed impression is the mirror image of the type.

SPACING THE WORDS *below*
The type on this modern composing stick shows how you could adjust the length of the line by inserting small pieces of metal between the words. These would not print because they are lower than the raised type.

Spacer

Adjustable grip to set length of line

Compositor setting type by hand

GUTENBERG'S WORKSHOP
Around 1438, Johannes Gutenberg invented a method of making type of individual letters from molten metal. The printers seen here are setting type and using the press in Gutenberg's workshop. Printed pages are hanging up for the ink to dry.

Screw locks type in place

Type forming a single page

HELD TIGHT
When the type was complete it was placed in a metal frame called a chase. The type was locked in place with pieces of wood or metal to make the form. The form was then placed in the printing press, inked, and printed.

Optical inventions

THE SCIENCE OF OPTICS is based on the fact that light rays are bent, or refracted, when they pass from one medium to another (for example, from air to glass). Egyptians knew the way in which curved pieces of glass (or lenses) refract light around the 8th century BCE. The Chinese learned their use in the 10th century CE. In 13th and 14th century Europe, the properties of lenses began to be used for improving vision, and eyeglasses, or spectacles, appeared. For thousands of years, people used mirrors (made at first of shiny metals) to see their faces. But it was not until the 17th century that more powerful optical instruments, capable of magnifying very small items and bringing distant objects into clearer focus, were made. Developments at this time included the telescope and the microscope, both of which were invented around 1600.

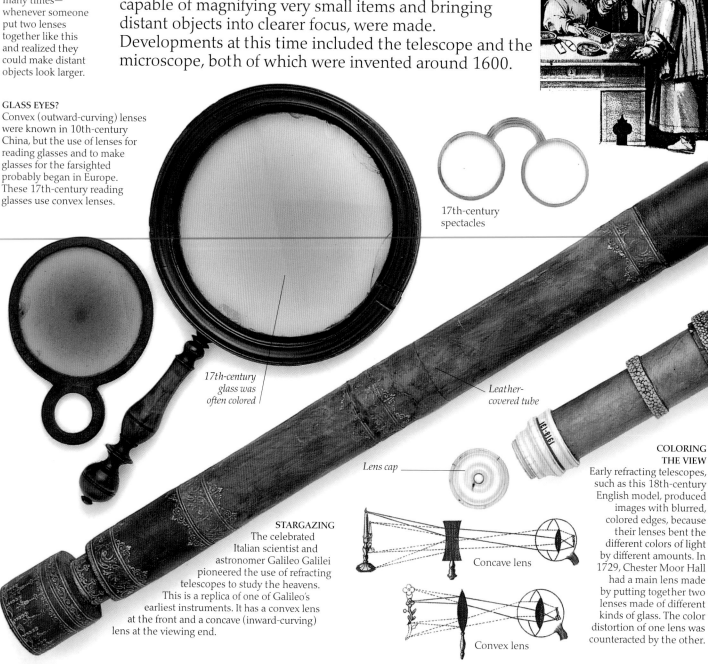

IN THE DISTANCE
The telescope must have been invented many times— whenever someone put two lenses together like this and realized they could make distant objects look larger.

GLASS EYES?
Convex (outward-curving) lenses were known in 10th-century China, but the use of lenses for reading glasses and to make glasses for the farsighted probably began in Europe. These 17th-century reading glasses use convex lenses.

BLURRED VISION
Spectacles, pairs of lenses for correcting sight defects, have been in use for more than 700 years. At first they were used only for reading and, like the ones being sold by this early optician, were perched on the nose when needed. Eyeglasses for correcting nearsightedness were first made in the 1450s.

17th-century spectacles

17th-century glass was often colored

Leather-covered tube

Lens cap

STARGAZING
The celebrated Italian scientist and astronomer Galileo Galilei pioneered the use of refracting telescopes to study the heavens. This is a replica of one of Galileo's earliest instruments. It has a convex lens at the front and a concave (inward-curving) lens at the viewing end.

Concave lens

Convex lens

COLORING THE VIEW
Early refracting telescopes, such as this 18th-century English model, produced images with blurred, colored edges, because their lenses bent the different colors of light by different amounts. In 1729, Chester Moor Hall had a main lens made by putting together two lenses made of different kinds of glass. The color distortion of one lens was counteracted by the other.

Eyepiece lens

Objective lens

COMPOUND INTEREST *above*
The compound microscope has not one, but two, lenses. The main lens magnifies the object, and the eyepiece lens enlarges the magnified image.

ANTON VAN LEEUWENHOEK
Dutchman Anton Van Leeuwenhoek taught himself to grind lenses and made simple microscopes with a tiny lens in a metal frame in the 17th century. Obtaining magnifications of up to 280 times, he was one of the first to study the miniature natural world and described "very little and odd animalcules" in drops of pondwater.

Lens cap

Lens cap

ON REFLECTION
The reflecting telescope uses a mirror lens. This prevents the problem of color distortion and the need for long focal-length lenses, which require long viewing tubes. This version has two mirrors and an eyepiece lens.

Wheel to adjust focus

Geared focusing mechanism

Lens

Light rays

A telescope forming an image using several lenses

Eyepiece

ON THE LEVEL
A quadrant and plumb line are attached to this 17th-century telescope. They help the astronomer work out the altitude of an object in the sky.

Plumb line

Quadrant

18th-century pocket telescope

Focus adjuster

PEEPING TOM
Jealousy glasses were sometimes used by the 18th-century gentry to keep an eye on one another. A mirror in the tube reflected the light rays so that you could look to one side when it seemed like you were looking straight ahead.

EYE-EYE, WHAT'S THAT?
Simple binoculars, such as these 19th-century opera glasses decorated with mother-of-pearl and enamel, consist of two telescopes mounted side by side. Prism binoculars had been invented by 1880. The prism, a wedge of glass, "folded" the light rays to shorten the length of the tube and allow greater magnification in a smaller instrument.

Calculating

Pᴇᴏᴘʟᴇ ʜᴀᴠᴇ ᴀʟᴡᴀʏs counted and calculated, but calculating became very important when the buying and selling of goods began. Aside from fingers, the first aids to counting and calculating were small pebbles, used to represent the numbers from one to 10. About 5,000 years ago, the Mesopotamians made several straight furrows in the ground into which the pebbles were placed. Simple calculations could be done by moving the pebbles from one furrow to another. Later, in China and Japan, the abacus was used in the same way, with its rows of beads representing hundreds, tens, and units. The next advances did not come until much later, with the invention of calculating aids such as logarithms, the slide rule, and basic mechanical calculators in the 17th century ᴄᴇ.

Upper beads are five times the value of lower beads

USING AN ABACUS
Experienced users can calculate at great speed with an abacus. As a result, this method of calculation has remained popular in China and Japan—even in the age of the electronic calculator.

POCKET CALCULATOR
The ancient Romans used a similar abacus to the Chinese. It had one bead on each rod in the upper part. These beads represented five times the value of the lower beads. This is a replica of a small Roman hand abacus made of brass.

THE ABACUS
In the Chinese abacus, there are five beads on the lower parts of each rod, each representing "1," and two beads on the upper part, each representing "5." The user moves the beads to perform calculations. The abacus is still used in China today.

HARD BARGAIN
Making quick calculations became important in the Middle Ages, when merchants began to trade all around Europe. The merchant in this Flemish painting is adding up the weight of a number of gold coins.

Parallel scales

KEEPING ACCOUNTS
On tally sticks, the figures were cut into the stick in the form of a series of notches. The stick was then split in two along its length, through the notches, so each person involved in the deal had a record.

Notches

USING LOGARITHMS *below*
A logarithm is an easy way of multiplying large numbers by adding smaller ones together. The slide rule, with its adjacent scales of numbers, works on this principle.

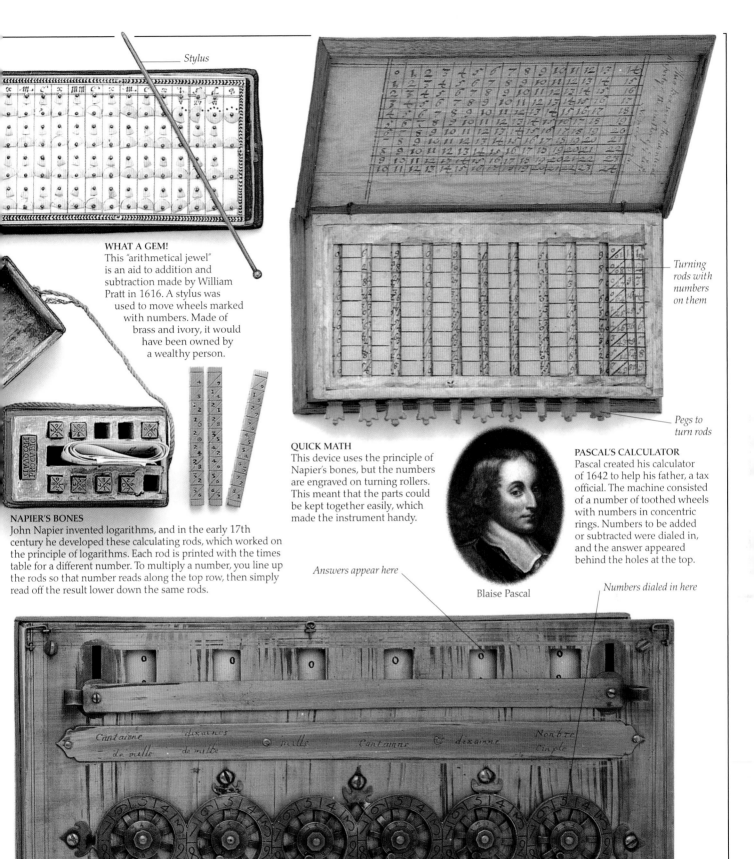

Stylus

WHAT A GEM!
This "arithmetical jewel"
is an aid to addition and
subtraction made by William
Pratt in 1616. A stylus was
used to move wheels marked
with numbers. Made of
brass and ivory, it would
have been owned by
a wealthy person.

Turning
rods with
numbers
on them

Pegs to
turn rods

QUICK MATH
This device uses the principle of
Napier's bones, but the numbers
are engraved on turning rollers.
This meant that the parts could
be kept together easily, which
made the instrument handy.

PASCAL'S CALCULATOR
Pascal created his calculator
of 1642 to help his father, a tax
official. The machine consisted
of a number of toothed wheels
with numbers in concentric
rings. Numbers to be added
or subtracted were dialed in,
and the answer appeared
behind the holes at the top.

Blaise Pascal

Answers appear here

Numbers dialed in here

NAPIER'S BONES
John Napier invented logarithms, and in the early 17th
century he developed these calculating rods, which worked on
the principle of logarithms. Each rod is printed with the times
table for a different number. To multiply a number, you line up
the rods so that number reads along the top row, then simply
read off the result lower down the same rods.

The steam engine

THE POWER DEVELOPED BY STEAM has fascinated people for hundreds of years. During the 1st century CE, Greek scientists realized that steam contained energy that could possibly be used by people. But the ancient Greeks did not use steam power to drive machinery. The first steam engines were designed at the end of the 17th century by engineers such as the Marquis of Worcester and Thomas Savery. Savery's engine was intended to be used for pumping water out of mines. The first really practical steam engine was designed by Thomas Newcomen, whose first engine appeared in 1712. Scottish instrument maker James Watt improved the steam engine still further. His engines condensed steam outside the main cylinder. By dispensing with the need alternately to heat and cool the cylinder, this saved heat. The engines also used steam to force the piston down, to increase efficiency. The new engines soon became a major source of power for factories and mines. Later developments included the more compact, high-pressure engine, which was used in locomotives and ships.

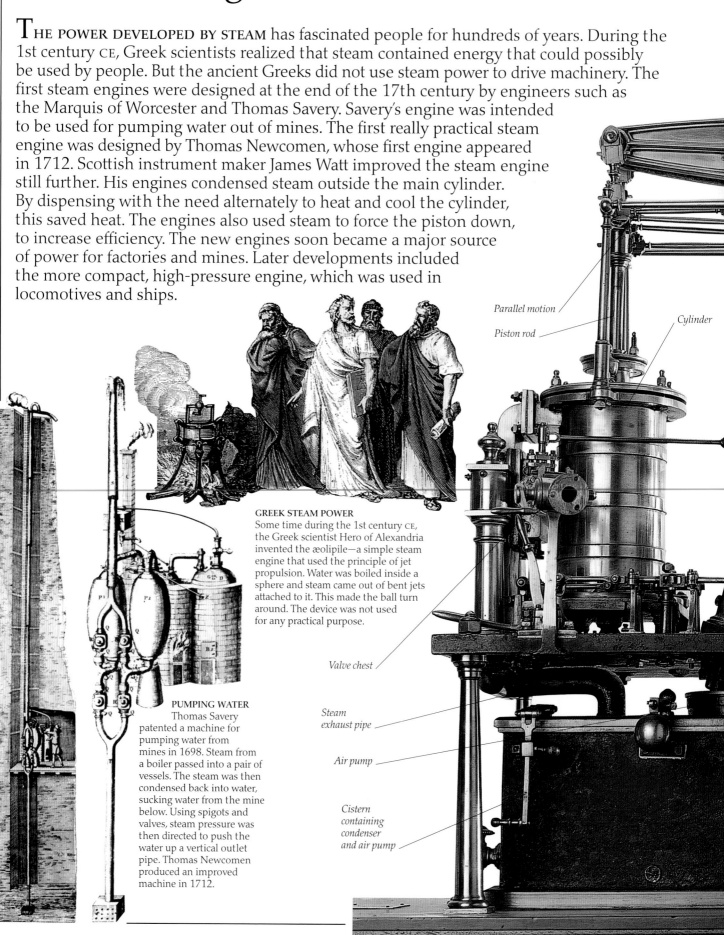

Parallel motion

Piston rod

Cylinder

GREEK STEAM POWER
Some time during the 1st century CE, the Greek scientist Hero of Alexandria invented the æolipile—a simple steam engine that used the principle of jet propulsion. Water was boiled inside a sphere and steam came out of bent jets attached to it. This made the ball turn around. The device was not used for any practical purpose.

Valve chest

Steam exhaust pipe

Air pump

Cistern containing condenser and air pump

PUMPING WATER
Thomas Savery patented a machine for pumping water from mines in 1698. Steam from a boiler passed into a pair of vessels. The steam was then condensed back into water, sucking water from the mine below. Using spigots and valves, steam pressure was then directed to push the water up a vertical outlet pipe. Thomas Newcomen produced an improved machine in 1712.

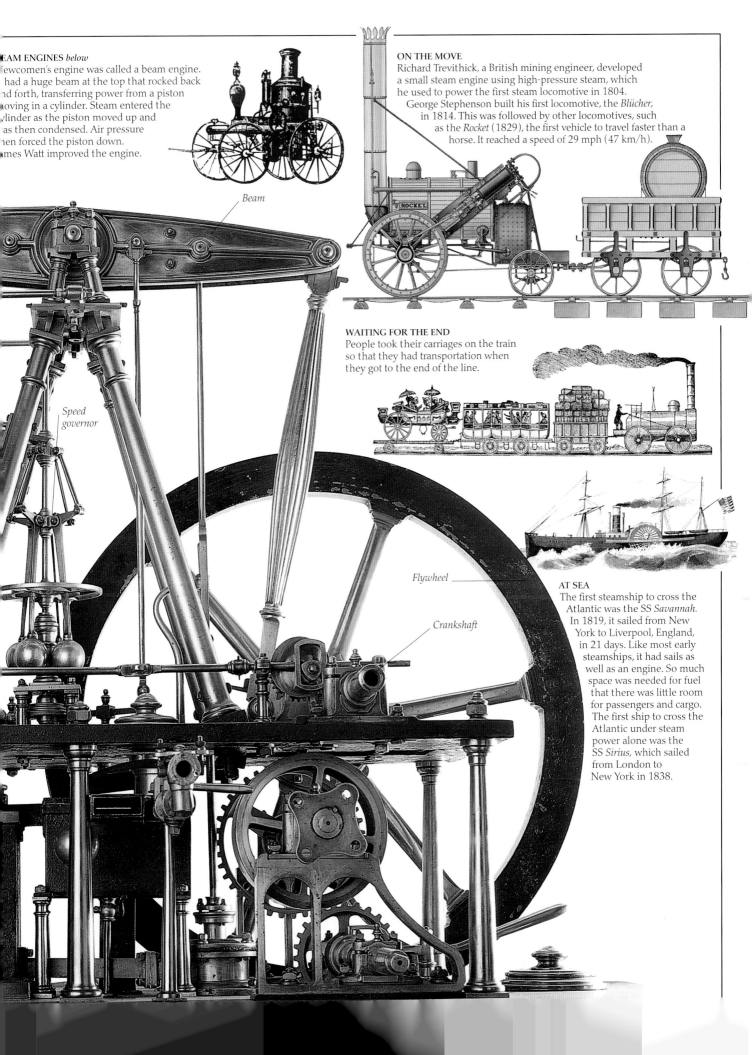

EAM ENGINES *below*
ewcomen's engine was called a beam engine.
had a huge beam at the top that rocked back
nd forth, transferring power from a piston
oving in a cylinder. Steam entered the
ylinder as the piston moved up and
as then condensed. Air pressure
hen forced the piston down.
mes Watt improved the engine.

Beam

Speed governor

ON THE MOVE
Richard Trevithick, a British mining engineer, developed
a small steam engine using high-pressure steam, which
he used to power the first steam locomotive in 1804.
George Stephenson built his first locomotive, the *Blücher*,
in 1814. This was followed by other locomotives, such
as the *Rocket* (1829), the first vehicle to travel faster than a
horse. It reached a speed of 29 mph (47 km/h).

ROCKET

WAITING FOR THE END
People took their carriages on the train
so that they had transportation when
they got to the end of the line.

Flywheel

Crankshaft

AT SEA
The first steamship to cross the
Atlantic was the SS *Savannah*.
In 1819, it sailed from New
York to Liverpool, England,
in 21 days. Like most early
steamships, it had sails as
well as an engine. So much
space was needed for fuel
that there was little room
for passengers and cargo.
The first ship to cross the
Atlantic under steam
power alone was the
SS *Sirius*, which sailed
from London to
New York in 1838.

Navigation and surveying

THE MORE PEOPLE TRAVELED by boat, the more important the skills of navigation became. Navigation probably originated on the Nile and Euphrates rivers about 5,000 years ago, when the Egyptians and Babylonians established trading routes. The Egyptians also pioneered surveying, essential for creating large buildings such as the pyramids. Navigation and surveying are related, because both deal with measuring angles and calculating long distances. From around 500 BCE, first the Greeks, then the Arabs and Indians, established astronomy, geometry, and trigonometry as sciences and created such instruments as the astrolabe and compass. Understanding the movements of heavenly bodies and the relationship between angles and distances, medieval seafarers were able to create a system of longitude and latitude for finding their way at sea without reference to landmarks. The Romans pioneered the widespread use of accurate surveying instruments, and Renaissance architects added the theodolite, our most important surveying tool.

Chinese mariner's compass

18th-century English compass

IN THE RIGHT DIRECTION
Magnetic compasses were used in Europe by about 1200 CE, but the Chinese are thought to have noticed about 1,500 years before that a suspended piece of lodestone (a magnetic iron mineral) points North-South.

Stones suspended from crossed sticks set at right angles to one another

RIGHT ANGLE *above*
Early surveyor's instruments such as the Egyptian *groma* were useful only on flat terrain and for setting a limited range of angles. With the *groma*, distant objects were marked out against the position of the stones in a horizontal plane.

Handle

STRETCHING IT OUT
Ropes, chains, tapes, and rods have all been used for measuring distance. In about 1620, Edmund Gunter developed this type of metal chain for determining the area of plots of land. The chain is 66 ft (20 m) long and is made of 100 links. Markers are placed at regular intervals.

Brass marker

OCTAN
In the 1730s, Englis seafarer John Hadle invented the octan This version is from about 1750. It enable navigators to measure th altitude of the Sun, Moo and stars so that the could find their latitud

Chain link

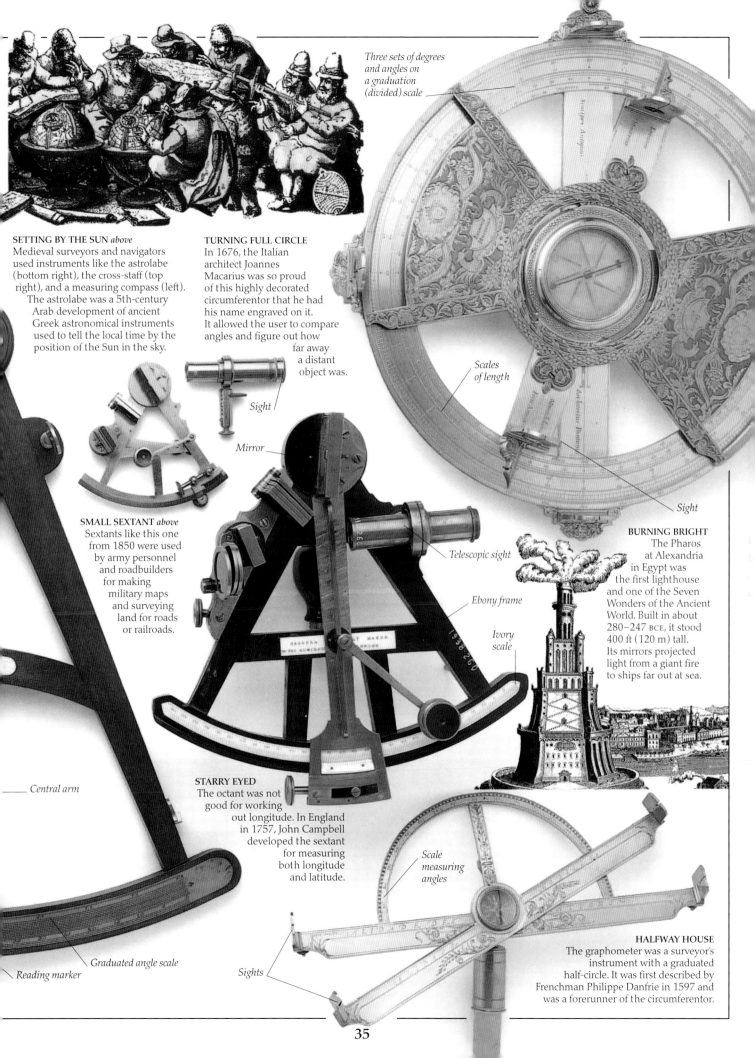

SETTING BY THE SUN *above*
Medieval surveyors and navigators
used instruments like the astrolabe
(bottom right), the cross-staff (top
right), and a measuring compass (left).
The astrolabe was a 5th-century
Arab development of ancient
Greek astronomical instruments
used to tell the local time by the
position of the Sun in the sky.

TURNING FULL CIRCLE
In 1676, the Italian
architect Joannes
Macarius was so proud
of this highly decorated
circumferentor that he had
his name engraved on it.
It allowed the user to compare
angles and figure out how
far away
a distant
object was.

*Three sets of degrees
and angles on
a graduation
(divided) scale*

*Scales
of length*

Sight

Sight

Mirror

SMALL SEXTANT *above*
Sextants like this one
from 1850 were used
by army personnel
and roadbuilders
for making
military maps
and surveying
land for roads
or railroads.

Telescopic sight

Ebony frame

*Ivory
scale*

BURNING BRIGHT
The Pharos
at Alexandria
in Egypt was
the first lighthouse
and one of the Seven
Wonders of the Ancient
World. Built in about
280–247 BCE, it stood
400 ft (120 m) tall.
Its mirrors projected
light from a giant fire
to ships far out at sea.

Central arm

STARRY EYED
The octant was not
good for working
out longitude. In England
in 1757, John Campbell
developed the sextant
for measuring
both longitude
and latitude.

*Scale
measuring
angles*

Graduated angle scale

Reading marker

Sights

HALFWAY HOUSE
The graphometer was a surveyor's
instrument with a graduated
half-circle. It was first described by
Frenchman Philippe Danfrie in 1597 and
was a forerunner of the circumferentor.

Spinning and weaving

EARLY PEOPLE used animal skins to help them keep warm, but about 10,000 years ago, people learned how to make cloth. Wool, cotton, flax, or hemp was first spun into a thin thread, using a spindle. The thread was then woven into a fabric. The earliest weaving machines probably consisted of little more than a pair of sticks that held a set of parallel threads, called the warp, while the cross-thread, called the weft, was inserted. Later machines, called looms, had rods that separated the threads to allow the weft to be inserted more easily. A piece of wood, known as the shuttle, held a spool of thread and was passed between the separated threads. The basic principles of spinning and weaving have stayed the same until the present day, although during the Industrial Revolution of the 18th century various ways were found of automating the processes. With new machines such as the spinning mule, many threads could be spun at the same time and, with the help of devices such as the flying shuttle, broad pieces of cloth could be woven very quickly.

MAKING CLOTH IN THE MIDDLE AGES
By about 1200–1300 CE, an improved loom was introduced to Europe from India. Called the horizontal loom, it had a framework of string or wire to separate the warp threads. The shuttle was passed across the loom by hand.

ANCIENT SPINDLE
Spindles such as this were turned by hand to twist the fibers and then allowed to hang so that the fibers were drawn into a thread. This example was found in 1921 at the ancient Egyptian site of Tel el Amarna.

SPINNING AT HOME
The spinning wheel, which was introduced to Europe from India about 1200 CE, speeded up the spinning process. In the 16th century, a foot treadle was added, freeing the spinner's hands—the left to draw out the fiber, the right to twist the thread.

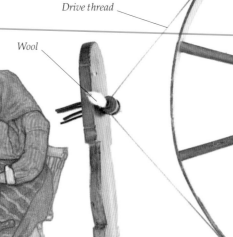

Drive thread

Wool

Wooden wheel

SPINNING WHEEL
This type of spinning wheel, called the great wheel, was used in homes until about 200 years ago. Spinning wheels like this produced a fine yarn of even thickness.

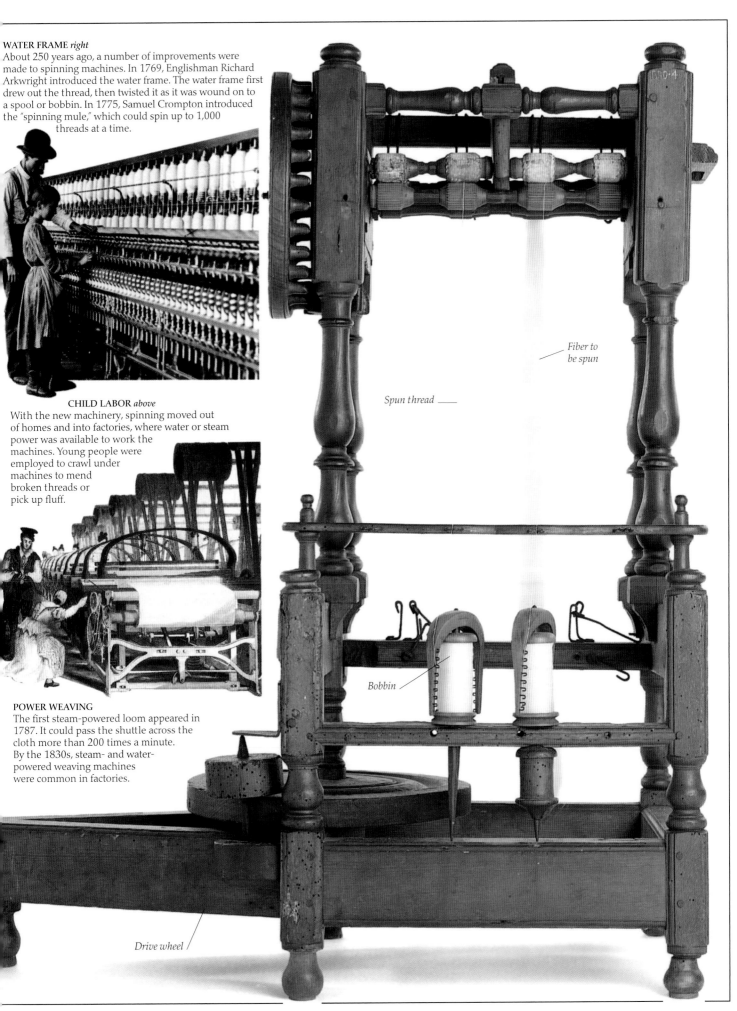

WATER FRAME *right*

About 250 years ago, a number of improvements were made to spinning machines. In 1769, Englishman Richard Arkwright introduced the water frame. The water frame first drew out the thread, then twisted it as it was wound on to a spool or bobbin. In 1775, Samuel Crompton introduced the "spinning mule," which could spin up to 1,000 threads at a time.

CHILD LABOR *above*

With the new machinery, spinning moved out of homes and into factories, where water or steam power was available to work the machines. Young people were employed to crawl under machines to mend broken threads or pick up fluff.

POWER WEAVING

The first steam-powered loom appeared in 1787. It could pass the shuttle across the cloth more than 200 times a minute. By the 1830s, steam- and water-powered weaving machines were common in factories.

Fiber to be spun

Spun thread

Bobbin

Drive wheel

Batteries

Over 2,000 years ago, the Greek scientist Thales produced small electric sparks by rubbing a cloth against amber, a yellow resin formed from the sap of long-dead trees. But it was a long time before people succeeded in harnessing this power to produce a battery—a device for producing a steady flow of electricity. It was in 1800 that Alessandro Volta published details of the first battery. Volta's battery produced electricity using the chemical reaction between certain solutions and metal electrodes. Other scientists, such as John Frederic Daniell, improved Volta's design by using different materials for the electrodes. Today's batteries follow the same basic design but use modern materials.

Metal electrodes

Fabric pads

VOLTA'S PILE *above*
Volta's battery, or "pile," consisted of disks of zinc and silver or copper separated by pads moistened with a weak acid or salt solution. Electricity flowed through a wire linking the top and bottom disks. An electrical unit, the volt, is named after Volta.

LIGHTNING FLASH
In 1752, American inventor Benjamin Franklin is said to have flown a kite in a thunderstorm. Electricity flowed down the wet line and produced a small spark, showing that lightning bolts were huge electric sparks.

ANIMAL ELECTRICITY
In 1771, Luigi Galvani found that the legs of dead frogs twitched when they were touched with metal rods. He thought the legs contained "animal electricity." Volta suggested a different explanation. Animals do produce electricity, but the twitching of the frogs' legs was probably caused by the metal rods and the moisture in the legs forming a simple cell.

Space filled with acid or solution

BUCKET CHEMISTRY
To produce higher voltages, and thus larger currents, many cells, each consisting of a pair of electrodes of different metals, were connected together. The common "voltaic" cell consists of copper and zinc electrodes immersed in weak acid. The English inventor William Cruickshank created this "trough" battery in 1800. The metal plates were soldered back-to-back and cemented into slots in a wooden case. The case was then filled with a dilute acid or a solution of ammonium chloride, a salt.

Zinc plate *Handles for lifting out zinc plates* *Copper plate*

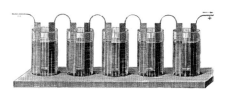

DIPPING IN, DRYING OUT
In about 1813, William Hyde Wollaston, an English chemist, created a battery like this. Zinc plates were fixed between the arms of U-shaped copper plates so that both sides of the zinc were used. The zinc plates were lifted out of the electrolyte solution to save zinc when the battery was not in use.

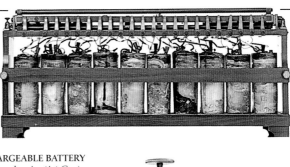

RELIABLE ELECTRICITY

The Daniell cell was the first reliable source of electricity. It produced a steady voltage over a considerable time. The cell has a copper electrode immersed in copper sulfate solution, and a zinc electrode in sulfuric acid. The liquids are kept separate by a porous pot.

Porous pot

Copper can acting
as electrode

Terminal

RECHARGEABLE BATTERY

The French scientist Gaston Planté invented the lead-acid accumulator in 1859, which can be recharged when it runs down. It has electrodes of lead and lead oxide in strong sulfuric acid.

Zinc rod electrode

WILHELM ROENTGEN right

The German scientist Wilhelm Roentgen discovered X-rays in 1895. Roentgen did not understand what these rays were so he named them X-rays.

GASSNER CELL left

Chemist Carl Gassner developed a pioneering type of "dry" cell in 1887. He used a zinc case as the negative (−) electrode, and a carbon rod as the positive (+) electrode. In between them was a paste of ammonium chloride solution and plaster of Paris.

HUBBLE BUBBLE right

Some early batteries used concentrated nitric acid but they gave off poisonous fumes. To avoid such hazards, the bichromate cell was developed in the 1850s. It used a glass flask filled with chromic acid. Zinc and carbon plates were used as electrodes.

POWERPACKS left

The so-called "dry" cell has a moist paste electrolyte inside a zinc container that acts as one electrode. The other electrode is manganese dioxide, connected via a carbon rod. Small modern batteries use a variety of materials for the electrodes. Mercury batteries were the first long-life dry cells. Most rechargeable batteries use lithium, the lightest of metals. They can be recharged hundreds of times and are used in laptops, cell phones, and portable music players.

Photography

THE INVENTION OF PHOTOGRAPHY made accurate images of any object rapidly available for the first time. It sprang from a combination of optics (see p. 28) and chemistry. The projection of the Sun's image on a screen had been explored by Arab astronomers in the 9th century CE, and by the Chinese before them. By the 16th century, Italian artists such as Canaletto were using lenses and a camera obscura to help them make accurate drawings. In 1725, a German professor, Johann Heinrich Schulze, showed that the darkening of silver nitrate solution when exposed to the Sun was caused by light, not heat. In 1827, a permanent visual record of an object was made by coating a metal plate with a light-sensitive material.

IN THE BLACK BOX
The camera obscura (from the Latin for dark room) was at first just a darkened room or large box with a tiny opening at the front and a screen or wall at the back onto which images were projected. From the 16th century, a lens was used instead of the "pinhole."

CALOTYPE IMAGE
By 1841, Englishman William Henry Fox Talbot had developed the Calotype. This is an early example. It was an improved version of a process he had announced two years before, within days of Daguerre's announcement. It provided a negative image, from which positives could be printed.

The daguerreotype

Nicéphore Niépce took the first surviving photograph. In 1825, he coated a pewter plate with bitumen and exposed it in a camera. Where light struck, the bitumen hardened. The unhardened areas were then dissolved away to leave a visible image. In 1839, his one-time partner, Louis-Jacques-Mandé Daguerre, developed a superior photographic process, producing the daguerreotype.

Lens cover

EXPOSING THE PLATE *below*
In some daguerreotype cameras, the object was viewed through a hole in the back of the box. Then the photographic plate, protected by a cover, was slid into place. The lens cap and the cover were removed to expose the plate, then replaced.

Lens with focusing control

Plate holder

DAGUERREOTYPE IMAGE
A daguerreotype was comprised of a copper plate coated with silver and treated with iodine vapor to make it sensitive to light. It was exposed in the camera, then the image was developed by mercury vapor and fixed with a strong solution of ordinary salt.

Aperture rings

MAKING ADJUSTMENTS
By using screw-in lens fittings and different-sized diaphragm rings to adjust the lens aperture, as on this folding daguerreotype camera of the 1840s, it became possible to photograph both close-up and distant objects in a variety of lighting conditions.

Lens and attachment

Folding daguerreotype camera

HEAVY LOADS
Enlargements could not be made with the early photographic processes, so for large pictures big glass plates were used. With a dark tent for inspecting wet plates as they were exposed, water, chemicals, and plates, the equipment could weigh more than 110 lb (50 kg).

The wet plate

From 1839 on, the pioneers of photography concentrated on the use of salts of silver as the light-sensitive material. In 1851, Frederick Scott Archer created a glass photographic plate more light-sensitive than its predecessors. It recorded negative images of fine detail with exposures of less than 30 seconds. The plate was coated with a chemical mix, put in the camera and exposed while still wet. It was messy, but gave excellent quality and much faster photos.

Plate holder

Chemicals for wet-plate process

Wet-plate negative

CHEMICALS *above right*
A wet-plate consisted of a glass sheet coated with silver salts and a sticky material called collodion. It was usually developed with pyrogallic acid and fixed with sodium thiosulphate ("hypo"). Chemicals were dispensed from small bottles.

IN AND OUT OF VIEW
This wet-plate camera was mounted on a tripod. The rear section into which the photographic plate was inserted could slide toward or away from the front lens section to increase or decrease the image size and produce a clear picture. Fine focusing was by means of a knob on the lens tube.

Moving on

In the 1870s, dry gelatine-coated plates covered with extremely light-sensitive silver bromide were developed. Soon, more sensitive paper allowed many prints to be made from a negative quickly and easily in a darkroom. In 1888, American George Eastman introduced a small, lightweight camera. It used film that came on a roll.

CANDID CAMERA *right*
By the 1920s, German optical instrument manufacturers such as Carl Zeiss were developing small precision cameras. This 1937 single-lens reflex (SLR) film camera is typical of those used until the 1990s, when digital cameras made film cameras obsolete.

Film winder

Viewfinder

Film winder

Lens

SLR camera

PHOTOGRAPHY FOR ALL
In the early 1900s, Eastman developed cheap Brownie box cameras such as this, and amateur photography was born. Each time a photo was taken, you would wind the film forward, ready for the next shot.

ROLL-FILM
Eastman's early roll-film consisted of a long thin strip of paper from which the negative coating was stripped and put down on glass plates before printing. In 1889, celluloid roll-film came on the market. The light-sensitive emulsion was coated onto a see-through base so that the stripping process was eliminated.

Medical inventions

PEOPLE HAVE ALWAYS practiced some form of medicine. Early peoples used herbs to cure illnesses. Some prehistoric skulls have been found with round holes, probably drilled with a trepan, a surgeon's circular saw. The ancient Greeks used this operation to relieve pressure on the brain after severe head injuries. The ancient Chinese practiced acupuncture, inserting needles into one part of the body to relieve pain or the symptoms of disease in another part. But until well into the 19th century, a surgeon's instruments differed little from early ones—scalpels, forceps, various hooks, saws, and other tools to perform amputations or to extract teeth. The first instruments used to determine the cause of illnesses were developed in Renaissance Europe following the pioneering anatomical work of scientists such as Leonardo da Vinci and Andreas Vesalius. In the 19th century, medicine developed quickly; many of the instruments still used in medicine and dentistry today, from stethoscopes to dental drills, were developed at this time.

PLUNGING IN
Syringes were first used in ancient India, China, and North Africa. Today, syringes consist of a hollow glass or plastic barrel and a plunger. A syringe equipped with a needle was first used around 1850 by French surgeon Charles Gabriel Pravaz to introduce fluids into veins.

Carbolic acid reservoir

Flexible rubber tube

Porcelain teeth

Mouthpiece placed over patient's mouth—has valves for breathing in and out

NUMBING PAIN
Before the introduction of anesthetics in 1846, surgery was done while the patient was still conscious and capable of feeling pain. To numb pain, nitrous oxide (laughing gas), ether, or chloroform were used. The gases were inhaled via a face mask.

Coiled spring

Ivory lower plate

YOU WON'T FEEL A THING
By the 1850s, anesthetics were used by dentists to "kill" pain. The first dental drills appeared in the 1860s.

Drill bit

DRILLING DOWN *right*
The Harrington "Erado" windup dental drill dates from about 1864. When fully wound, it worked for up to 2 minutes.

FIRM BITE *above*
The first full set of false teeth similar to those used today was made in France in the 1780s. This set of partial dentures dates from about 1860.

SPRAY IT ON *left*
By 1865, Scottish surgeon Joseph Lister had developed an antiseptic carbolic steam spray. It created a mist of carbolic acid intended to kill germs around the operation site. This version dates from about 1875.

Candle

DOWN THE TUBE
In 1816, French physician René Laënnec created a tube through which he could hear the patient's heartbeat.

Ivory earpiece

THROUGH THE LOOKING TUBE *right*
Different types of endoscope, for viewing inside the body without surgery, were developed in the 19th century. This 1880s version used a candle as a light source.

Speculum placed in patient's ear

Funnel for concentrating light

Viewing lens

LISTENING IN
Laënnec's single-tube stethoscope was later developed into this 1855 version of the present-day design, with two earpieces. The stethoscope can be used to listen to the sounds made by the heart, lungs, or blood vessels, or to the heartbeat of a baby in the womb.

TAKING THE PULSE *left*
In the early 17th century, physician William Harvey was the first to show how blood circulated around the body. But it was not until much later that the link between the pulse, heart activity, and health was established.

Metal tubes (modern tubes are plastic), for transmitting the sounds

Ether vapor outlet valve

Air inlet valve

UNDER PRESSURE *above*
Blood pressure is measured by feeling the pulse and slowly applying a measured force to the skin until the pulse disappears. The instrument to do this was invented by Samuel von Basch and called a sphygmomanometer.

HOT UNDER THE COLLAR? *right*
These thermometers, from about 1865, were placed in the mouth (straight version) or under the armpit (curved-end type). Measuring the patient's temperature was not common practice until the early 20th century.

Temperature scale in degrees Fahrenheit

Cone

Reservoir of mercury

Ether-soaked sponges

LIGHT-HEADED FEELING
In the 19th century, ether was used as an anesthetic. The "Letheon" ether inhaler of 1847 comprised a glass jar filled with ether-soaked sponges through which air was drawn as the patient breathed in.

R 1978/1936

A625399

HOLLOW SOUNDS
The disk-shaped sound collector on this 1830s stethoscope would have been used to listen to high-pitched sounds, like those made by the lungs, rather than low-pitched ones, which heartbeats produce.

Kink in tube—to give good fit in armpit

The telephone

FOR CENTURIES, people have tried to send signals over long distances, using bonfires and flashing mirrors to transmit messages. It was Frenchman Claude Chappe who in 1793 devised the word "telegraph" (literally, writing at a distance) to describe his message machine. Moving arms mounted on towertops signaled numbers and letters. Over the next 40 years, electric telegraphs were developed. In 1876, Alexander Graham Bell patented the telephone, enabling speech to be sent along wires for the first time. Bell's work with the deaf led to an interest in how sounds are produced by vibrations in the air. His research on a device called the "harmonic telegraph" led him to discover that an electric current could be changed to resemble the vibrations made by a speaking voice. This was the principle on which his work on the telephone was based.

OPENING SPEECH
Alexander Graham Bell developed the telephone after working with deaf people as a speech teacher. Here he is making the first call on the New York to Chicago line.

ALL-IN-ONE
Early models such as Bell's "Box telephone" of 1876–77 had a trumpetlike mouthpiece and earpiece combined. The instrument contains a membrane that vibrated when someone spoke into the mouthpiece. The vibrations created a varying electric current in a wire, and the receiver turned the varying current back into vibrations that you could hear.

Magnet *Earpiece and mouthpiece combined*

Wire coil *Iron diaphragm*

EARPIECE
In this earpiece of about 1878 a fluctuating electric current passing through the wire coil made the iron diaphragm move to make sounds.

Telegraph

The forerunner of the telephone, the telegraph allowed signals to be sent along a wire. The first telegraphs were used on the railroads to help keep track of trains. Later, telegraph wire linked major cities.

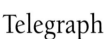

MESSAGE MACHINES
With the Morse key (left) you could send signals made up of short dots and long dashes. In the Cooke and Wheatstone system (right) the electric current made needles point at different letters.

DON'T HANG UP
In 1877, Thomas Edison developed different mouthpiece and earpiece units. Models such as this were hung from a special switch that disconnected the line on closing.

WIRED FOR SOUND
Some early telegraph cables used copper wires sheathed in glass. Overhead telegraph and phone wires used iron for strength.

EASY LISTENING
This wall-mounted telephone of 1879 was invented by Thomas Edison and has a microphone and receiver of his design. The user had to wind the handle while listening. A ring of the bell indicated an incoming call or a successful connection.

Earpiece

REPEAT THAT NUMBER
The earliest telephone exchanges were manual. An operator took your number and the number you wanted. Then he or she plugged the wire from your phone into a "switchboard" to make a complete electrical circuit connection to the other phone.

HANDSETS
By 1885, the transmitter and receiver had been combined to form a handset. At first this was metal, but by 1929 plastic handsets were common.

Mouthpiece

Mouthpiece

Hook for earpiece

Transmitter containing carbon granules, compressed and released by sound waves to create an electric current of varying strength

IT'S A STICKUP
Some candlestick-shaped phones of the 1920s and 1930s had a dial for calling numbers via an automatic exchange.

Numbered dial

arpiece

LONG DISTANCE CALL FOR YOU
"Cradle" telephones like this were popular by the 1890s. This one dates from 1937, by which time there was a transatlantic telephone service between London and New York.

Drawer for directory

45

Recording

Sᴏᴜɴᴅs ᴡᴇʀᴇ ʀᴇᴄᴏʀᴅᴇᴅ for the first time in 1877 on an experimental machine that Thomas Edison (1847–1931) hoped would translate telephone calls into telegraph messages. It recorded the calls as indentations in a strip of paper passing under a stylus. Edison noticed that when he passed the indented paper through the machine again, he heard a faint echo of the original sound. This mechanical way of recording sound continued until electrical systems appeared in the 1920s. Magnetic principles were used to develop tape-recording systems. These received a commercial boost, first in 1935, with the development of magnetic plastic tape and then, in the 1960s, with the arrival of microelectronics (p. 62).

TWO-IN-ONE MACHINE

By 1877, Edison had created separate devices for recording and playing back. Sounds made into a horn caused its diaphragm to vibrate and its stylus to create indentations on a thin sheet of tinfoil wrapped around the recording drum. Putting the playback stylus and its diaphragm in contact with the foil and rotating the drum reproduced the sounds via a second diaphragm.

Mouthpiece (horn not shown)

Drive axle, threaded to move length of foil beneath fixed stylus

Tinfoil was wrapped around this brass drum

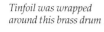

Cross section showing needle on cylinder

Edison phonograph showing positions of needle and horn

Position of horn

Wooden horn

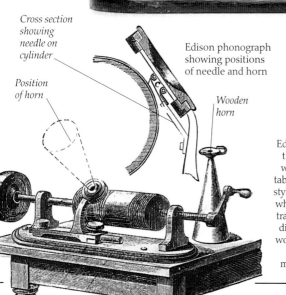

PLAY IT AGAIN, SAM

To play back sound with Edison's machine, you replaced the mouthpiece with a large wooden horn (shown on the table at the back). This pressed a stylus (steel needle) into the foil, which picked up vibrations and transferred them to a thin, iron diaphragm. As the diaphragm wobbled back and forth, similar to a vibrating drumskin, it made sounds you could hear.

Early recording session

46

Cylinder
and box

IN THE GROOVE *above*
Edison eventually used a continuous groove in a wax cylinder, the depth of which varied with the intensity of the sound being recorded. These later cylinder recordings lasted for up to four minutes.

78 rpm
shellac disc

ON THE FLAT
In 1887, Emile Berliner created the forerunner of modern records (discs) and record players. The playback mechanisms were similar to their predecessors, but instead of a cylinder Berliner used a flat disc with a groove that varied not in depth but in side-to-side movement.

CUTTING A DISC *above*
Berliner's first disc system used a glass disc coated with soft wax as a "negative." This was used to photo-engrave the recording pattern on to flat metal disc "positives." In 1895, he developed a method of printing plastic records in large quantities: shellac positives, like this 78 rpm disc, were pressed from a nickel-plated negative.

Needles

WAXING LYRICAL *left*
Edison's tinfoil recordings played for only about a minute and were soon worn out by the steel needles. In the mid 1880s, Chichester Bell, cousin of Alexander Graham Bell, with scientist Charles Tainter, used a sapphire stylus and developed a wax-coated cylinder as a more durable alternative. Edison created this version in about 1905.

Horn to channel sounds from the iron diaphragm

Steel needle

Turntable

Tape recording

In 1898, Danish inventor Valdemar Poulsen produced the first magnetic recorder. Recordings were made on steel piano wire. In the 1930s, two German companies, Telefunken and I. G. Farben, developed a plastic tape coated with magnetic iron oxide, and this soon replaced steel wires and paper tapes.

WIRED UP *left*
This 1903 Poulsen telegraphone was electrically driven and replayed. The machine was used primarily for dictation and telephone message work. The sounds were recorded on wire.

ON TAPE *above*
This tape recorder of about 1950 has three heads, one to erase previous recordings, one to record, and the third to replay.

The internal combustion engine

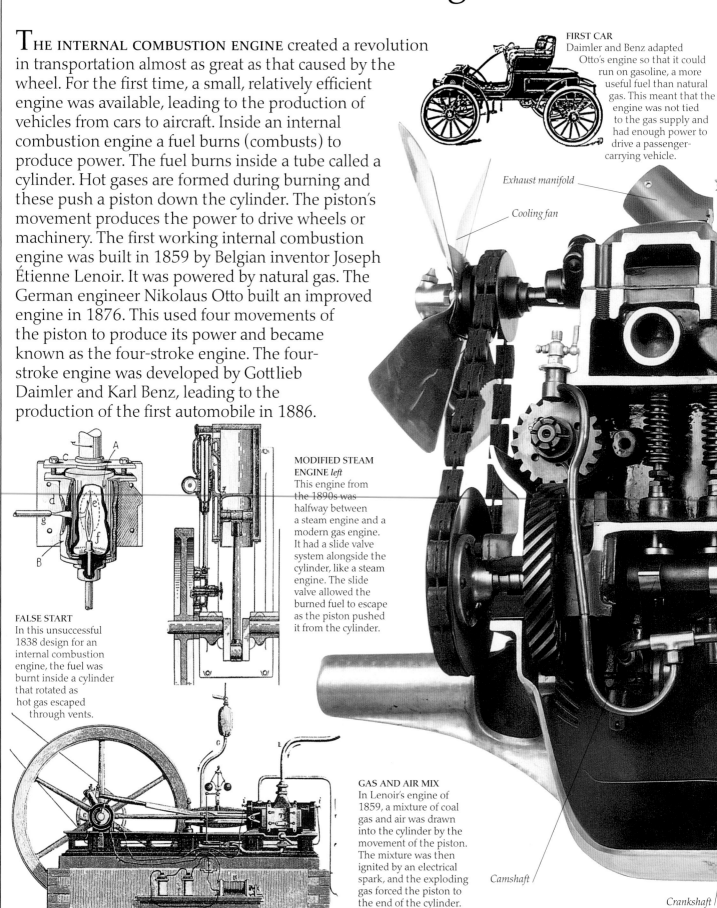

THE INTERNAL COMBUSTION ENGINE created a revolution in transportation almost as great as that caused by the wheel. For the first time, a small, relatively efficient engine was available, leading to the production of vehicles from cars to aircraft. Inside an internal combustion engine a fuel burns (combusts) to produce power. The fuel burns inside a tube called a cylinder. Hot gases are formed during burning and these push a piston down the cylinder. The piston's movement produces the power to drive wheels or machinery. The first working internal combustion engine was built in 1859 by Belgian inventor Joseph Étienne Lenoir. It was powered by natural gas. The German engineer Nikolaus Otto built an improved engine in 1876. This used four movements of the piston to produce its power and became known as the four-stroke engine. The four-stroke engine was developed by Gottlieb Daimler and Karl Benz, leading to the production of the first automobile in 1886.

FIRST CAR
Daimler and Benz adapted Otto's engine so that it could run on gasoline, a more useful fuel than natural gas. This meant that the engine was not tied to the gas supply and had enough power to drive a passenger-carrying vehicle.

Exhaust manifold

Cooling fan

MODIFIED STEAM ENGINE *left*
This engine from the 1890s was halfway between a steam engine and a modern gas engine. It had a slide valve system alongside the cylinder, like a steam engine. The slide valve allowed the burned fuel to escape as the piston pushed it from the cylinder.

FALSE START
In this unsuccessful 1838 design for an internal combustion engine, the fuel was burnt inside a cylinder that rotated as hot gas escaped through vents.

GAS AND AIR MIX
In Lenoir's engine of 1859, a mixture of coal gas and air was drawn into the cylinder by the movement of the piston. The mixture was then ignited by an electrical spark, and the exploding gas forced the piston to the end of the cylinder.

Camshaft

Crankshaft

FOUR-STROKE CYCLE

During the induction stroke, the piston moves down, sucking the fuel-air mixture into the cylinder through the open inlet valve. During the compression stroke, the piston moves up to compress the mixture; the spark plug ignites the mixture at the top of the stroke. During the "power" stroke, the expanding gases (the burning fuel) push the piston down. During the exhaust stroke, the piston moves up, forcing the hot gases out through the open exhaust valve.

Induction   Compression   Power   Exhaust

CAR OF THE PEOPLE *right*

The 1908 Model T Ford was the first car to be mass-produced. Over 15 million were made before production ended in 1927. By 1910, the main features of many later cars had been established: a four-stroke engine mounted at the front, with power being transmitted to the rear wheels via a drive shaft.

Valve

Cylinder

Piston

Gudgeon

Connecting rod

Clutch

INSIDE AN ENGINE

This 1925 Morris engine is a basic power unit for a family car. Its four in-line cylinders have aluminum pistons. The valves are opened by push rods operated by a camshaft and closed by springs. Power is transmitted via the crankshaft to the gearbox. The clutch disconnects the engine from the gearbox when the driver changes gear.

Movies

In 1824, an English doctor, Peter Mark Roget, first explained the phenomenon of "persistence of vision." He noticed that if you see an object in a series of closely similar positions in a rapid sequence, your eyes tend to see a single moving object. It did not take people long to realize that a moving image could be created with a series of still images, and within 10 years scientists all over the world were developing a variety of devices for creating this illusion.

Most of these machines remained little more than novelties or toys but, combined with improvements in illumination systems for magic lanterns and with developments in photography, they helped the progress of movie technology. The first successful public showing of moving images created by cinematography was in the 1890s by two French brothers, Auguste and Louis Lumière. They created a combined camera and projector, the Cinématographe, that recorded the pictures on a celluloid strip.

ROUND AND ROUND
In 1879, British photographer Eadweard Muybridge designed the zoopraxiscope for projecting moving images on a screen. The images were a sequence of pictures based on photographs, painted on a glass disk that rotated to create a moving picture.

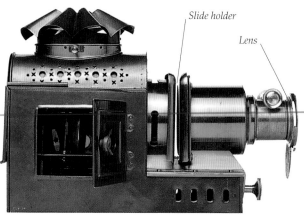

Slide holder

Lens

MAGIC LIGHT SHOW *above*
In a magic lantern, images on a transparent slide are projected on a screen using a lens and a light source. Early magic lanterns used a candle; later, limelight or carbon arcs were used to give more intense illumination.

MOVING PICTURES
The Lumière brothers opened the world's first movie theater in 1896. Their Cinématographe worked like a magic lantern, but projected images from a continuous strip of film.

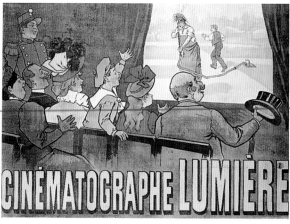

SILVER SCREEN
The Lumières' system was used for the first regular movie showings in Europe. The brothers opened a movie theater in a café basement in 1895.

Lens hood to keep stray light from reaching lens

An early moviemaker at work

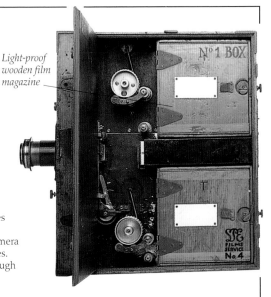

MOVEMENT *above*
In the 1880s, Muybridge produced thousands of sequences of photographs that showed animals and people in motion. He placed 12 or more cameras side by side and used electromagnetic shutters that fired at precise, split-second intervals as the subject moved in front of them.

LONG AND WINDING PATH *right*
Movie film must be wound through the camera and projector at between 16 and 24 frames a second. Many feet of film are needed for shows lasting more than a few minutes. This English camera from 1909 had two 400-ft (120-m) film magazines. Film comes out of the first magazine, passes through the gate, and is fed into the lower magazine.

Light-proof wooden film magazine

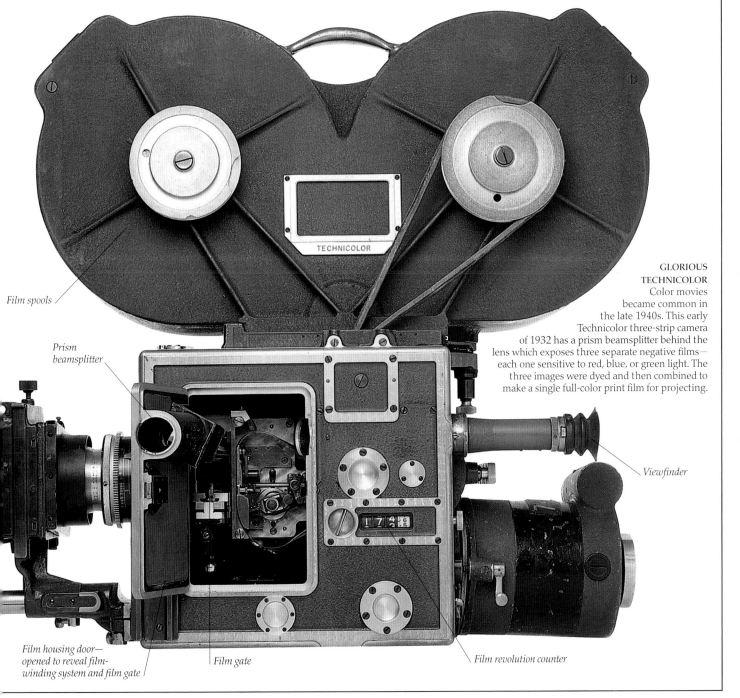

Film spools

Prism beamsplitter

GLORIOUS TECHNICOLOR
Color movies became common in the late 1940s. This early Technicolor three-strip camera of 1932 has a prism beamsplitter behind the lens which exposes three separate negative films—each one sensitive to red, blue, or green light. The three images were dyed and then combined to make a single full-color print film for projecting.

Viewfinder

Film housing door—opened to reveal film-winding system and film gate

Film gate

Film revolution counter

Radio

GUGLIELMO MARCONI, experimenting in his parents' attic near Bologna, Italy, developed the first radio. Fascinated by the idea of using radio waves to send messages through the air, he created an invention that was to change the world, making wireless communication over long distances possible and transforming the entertainment business. For a transmitter he used an electric spark generator invented by Heinrich Hertz. Radio waves from this were detected by a "coherer," the invention of Frenchman Edouard Branly. The coherer turned the radio waves into an electric current. In 1894, Marconi made an electric bell ring by sending radio signals across the room. Within eight years he was sending radio messages 3,000 miles (4,800 km) across the Atlantic.

JUMPING JACK FLASH *above*
In 1888, German physicist Heinrich Hertz made an electric spark jump between pairs of metal spheres, creating a current in a circuit nearby. Hertz was studying electromagnetic waves, a type of radiation that includes visible light, radio waves, X-rays, infrared waves, and ultraviolet light.

Glass bulb

Positive electrode (anode)

Grid

Filament (negative electrode – cathode)

Diode

Triode

HEATING UP
Early radio receivers were not sensitive. In 1904, Englishman John Ambrose Fleming first used a diode (a device with two electrodes) as a better detector of radio waves. It was a type of thermionic valve (from the Greek "therm," meaning heat and "ion," the electrically charged particles of atoms). Diodes convert alternating electric currents into direct ones for use in electric circuits.

CARRIER WAVES
Thermionic valves developed into the triode of 1906, with a third electrode, the grid, between the cathode and anode. Triodes allow telephone messages and microphone signals to be amplified. The amplified signals are combined with special radio waves known as carrier waves so that they can be transmitted over great distances.

IT'S THE CAT'S WHISKERS
When radio stations first started broadcasting in the early 1920s, listeners tuned in using receivers made of silicon crystals or lead compounds and thin wires popularly known as cat's whiskers. The radio signals were weak, so headphones were used. Headphones use magnets, coils of wire, and paper cones to convert electric signals back into the sound of radio broadcasts.

ACROSS THE AIRWAVES
Marconi developed radio as the first practical system of wireless telegraphy, which made possible uninterrupted communication over land and sea.

Electrical connections to battery

HEAVY SOUNDS
Valves and other radio components needed a direct current supply. Because household electricity was not widespread until the 1940s, radio sets of the 1930s and 1940s ran off large, powerful batteries. The resulting radio receiver was big and heavy. A separate loudspeaker was used with this model.

Tuning condenser

Coils

Valve

Power supply

Crystal

Cat's whisker

Tuning dials

Volume control

WHAT THE WHISKER DID
The crystal detector only worked when the cat's whisker made precise contact with the crystal. It was often a problem establishing the contact, so crystal sets were difficult to use. They were soon superseded by sets using thermionic valves.

WORDS AND PICTURES
In the 1920s, valves such as this triode not only enabled the first speech broadcast from England to Australia—by Marconi in 1924—but also in the development of television cameras, transmitters, and receivers.

GOOD RECEPTION
This early valve receiver had a loudspeaker built into the cabinet.

Plug-in base

RADIO COMES TO EVERY HOME
By the 1920s, many radio transmitters had been built and radio was within reach of many households in Europe and the US.

GATHER ROUND
This detail from a painting by W. R. Scott shows people gathering around a radio receiver at a Christmas party. In 1922, when this picture was painted, radio was still a new attraction for most people.

Inventions in the home

Scientist Michael Faraday discovered how to generate electricity in 1831. But it was many years before electricity was used around the home. At first, large houses and factories installed their own generators and used electricity for lighting. The electric filament lamp was demonstrated in 1879. In 1882, the first large electricity power station was built in New York City. Gradually, as people began to realize how appliances could save work in the home, mechanical items, such as early vacuum cleaners, were replaced by more efficient electrical versions. As the middle classes came to rely less and less on domestic servants, labor-saving appliances became more popular. Electric motors were applied to food mixers and hair dryers around 1920. Electric kettles, stoves, and heaters, making use of the heating effect of an electric current, had also appeared by this time. Some of these items were very similar in design to those used today.

WATER CLOSET
The first description of a flush toilet or "water closet" was published by Sir John Harington in 1596. But the idea did not catch on widely until household drainage systems were installed in major cities. London's system, for example, was not in operation until the 1860s. By this time several improved versions of the "W.C." had been patented.

KEEPING COOL
Electric refrigerators became popular in the 1920s. They revolutionized food storage.

TEATIME
In the automatic tea maker of 1902, levers, springs, and the steam from the kettle activate stages in the tea-making process. A bell is struck to tell you that the tea is ready.

BOILING POINT
The Swan electric kettle of 1921 was the first with a totally immersed heating element. Earlier models had elements in a separate compartment in the bottom of the kettle that wasted a lot of heat.

THE "WILSON" COOKER is Perfection for Baking Bread Pastry and TEA CAKES

COOK'S FRIEND
Before the 19th century, you had to light a fire to cook food. By 1879, an electric stove had been designed in which food was heated by electricity passing through insulated wire wound around the cooking pot. In the 1890s, heating elements were made as iron plates with wires beneath. The modern element, which can be bent to any shape, came into use in the 1920s.

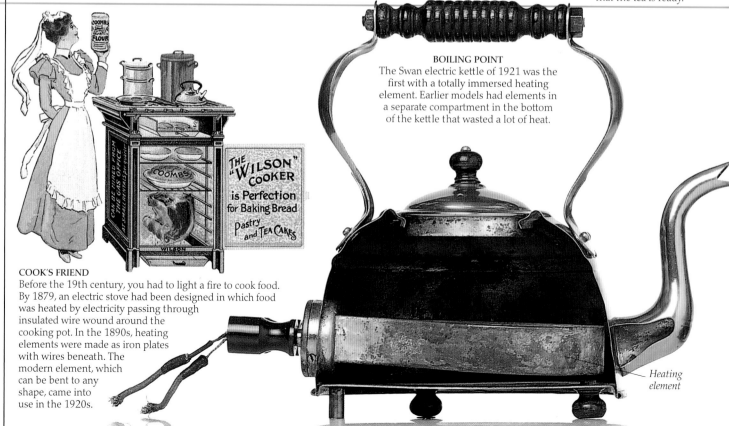

Heating element

EASY MIXING
The 1918 food mixer had two blades driven by an electric motor. A hinge allowed the mixer to be turned to a horizontal position.

Dowsing bulb

Electric motor

GOOD GROOMING
The 1925 electric hair dryer had a simple heater and a small fan. It was made of aluminum with a wooden handle. A switch gave two levels of heat.

KEEPING WARM
Early electric fires used the Dowsing bulb. This was like an oversized lightbulb that was coated on the outside and mounted in front of a reflector in an attempt to concentrate the heat given off.

Heating element

ELECTRIC IRON
The first electric iron was heated by an electric arc between carbon rods and was highly dangerous. A safer iron was patented in 1882. It used an electrically heated wire element like a hot plate.

THE SAD IRON *left*
The most common form of iron in use from the 18th century until the early 20th century was the sad iron ("sad" meant heavy). These were used in pairs, with one heating up over the embers of a fire while the other was being used.

Bellows

QUICK COOKING *left*
The pressure cooker was invented by Frenchman Denis Papin in 1679. He called it the "new digester." Superheated steam at high pressure formed inside the strong container. The high temperature cooked the food in a very short time.

CLEANING UP *right*
The mechanical vacuum cleaner of the early 20th century required two people to operate it. A bellows was worked by a wooden handle, sucking in dirt. American William H. Hoover began to make electric cleaners in 1908.

The cathode ray tube

IN 1887, PHYSICIST William Crookes was investigating the properties of electricity. He used a glass tube containing two metal plates, the electrodes. When a high voltage was applied and the air pumped out of the tube, electricity passed between the electrodes and caused a glow in the tube. As the pressure fell (approaching a vacuum) the light went out, yet the glass itself glowed. Crookes called the rays that caused this cathode rays; they were, in fact, an invisible flow of electrons. Later, Ferdinand Braun created a tube with an end wall coated with a substance that glowed when struck by cathode rays. This was the forerunner of the modern TV receiver tube.

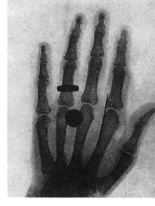

HANDS ON
Wilhelm Roentgen discovered X-rays using a similar tube to Crookes' in 1895.

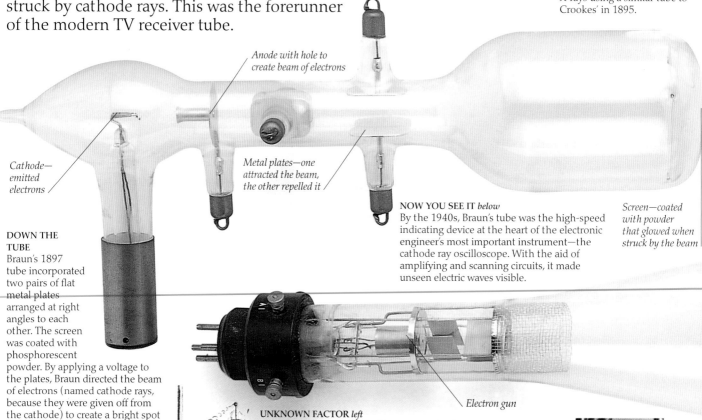

Anode with hole to create beam of electrons

Cathode— emitted electrons

Metal plates—one attracted the beam, the other repelled it

Screen—coated with powder that glowed when struck by the beam

DOWN THE TUBE
Braun's 1897 tube incorporated two pairs of flat metal plates arranged at right angles to each other. The screen was coated with phosphorescent powder. By applying a voltage to the plates, Braun directed the beam of electrons (named cathode rays, because they were given off from the cathode) to create a bright spot of light on the screen. By varying the voltage across the plates, he made the spot move around.

NOW YOU SEE IT *below*
By the 1940s, Braun's tube was the high-speed indicating device at the heart of the electronic engineer's most important instrument—the cathode ray oscilloscope. With the aid of amplifying and scanning circuits, it made unseen electric waves visible.

Electron gun

UNKNOWN FACTOR *left*
German physicist Wilhelm Roentgen noticed that as well as cathode rays, another form of radiation was emitted from a discharge tube when very high voltages were used. Unlike cathode rays, these rays, which he called "X" for "unknown," were not deflected by electrically charged plates nor by magnets. They passed through materials and darkened photographic plates.

Induction coil to produce high voltage

Photographic plate recording X-rays passing through a hand

IN A SPIN *right*
In 1884, Paul Nipkow invented a system of spinning disks with spirals of holes to transform an object into an image on a screen. In 1925, Scottish inventor John Logie Baird (standing in the picture) used Nipkow disks, not a cathode ray tube, to give the world's first demonstration of television.

Electromagnetic coil to direct electron beams

Single-beam gun

CHEAPER TV
In the late 1960s, the Japanese firm Sony developed and patented the Trinitron system, a cathode ray tube with a different design from RCA's original color tube. This meant that Sony did not have to pay fees to RCA for every tube it made.

Electron gun producing three separate beams

Trinitron tube

TV screen

FASTER THAN THE EYE CAN NOTICE *below*
Until the 1960s, most home television receivers produced black-and-white pictures and operated with valves (p. 52). The "tube" consisted of a single electron gun producing a beam that was made to scan the screen up to 50 times a second. Tubes gradually got shorter, so TVs became smaller.

Phosphor screen

LEVISION GOES PUBLIC
1936, the BBC started the first public high-definition
evision service from this studio at Alexandra Palace,
ndon. At first it used both Baird's system and
e using the cathode ray tube. The latter gave the
st results and Baird's system was never used again.
1939, RCA (Radio Corporation of America) started
e first fully electronic television
rvice in the United States.

IN FRONT OF THE BOX *above*
Early television sets, such as this RCA Victor model, had small screens but contained such a mass of additional components that they were housed in large boxes. At the time, many such sets cost as much as a small car.

Electron gun

Electron beam

Flight

THE FIRST CREATURES to fly in a man-made craft were a rooster, a duck, and a sheep. They were sent up in a hot-air balloon made by the French Montgolfier brothers in September 1783. When the animals landed safely, the brothers were encouraged to send two of their friends, Pilâtre de Rozier and the Marquis d'Arlandes, on a 25-minute flight over Paris. Among the earliest pioneers of powered flight were Englishmen William Henson and John Stringfellow, who built a model aircraft powered by a steam engine in the 1840s. The engine was heavy and had low power but the craft did have many of the features of the successful airplane. It was the American Wright brothers who first achieved powered, controlled flight in a full-sized airplane. Their *Wright Flyer* of 1903 was powered by a lightweight gasoline engine.

AIRBORNE CARRIAGE
Henson and Stringfellow's "Aerial steam carriage" had many features that were taken up by later aircraft designers. It had a separate tail with rudders and elevators and upward-sloping wings. The craft looks strange, but it was a surprisingly practical design.

Wooden and canvas wing

MECHANICAL WING
Some 500 years ago, Leonardo da Vinci designed a number of flying machines. These mostly had mechanical flapping wings. They were bound to fail because of the great effort needed to flap the wings; da Vinci also designed a simple helicopter.

FIRST FLIGHT
On June 4, 1783, Joseph and Etienne Montgolfier demonstrated a paper-lined silk hot-air balloon. It climbed to about 3,300 ft (1,000 m). Later in the same year, the brothers sent up animal and human passengers.

INVENTEURS
MONTGOLFIER
Ballon
Cailler's CHOCOLATS FINS
Série XXI   N.º 3

GLIDING FREE
The first piloted glider was built by German engineer Otto Lilienthal. He made many flights between 1891 and 1896, when he was killed as his glider crashed. His work showed the basics of controlling a craft in the air.

Otto Lilienthal with one of his gliders in 1896

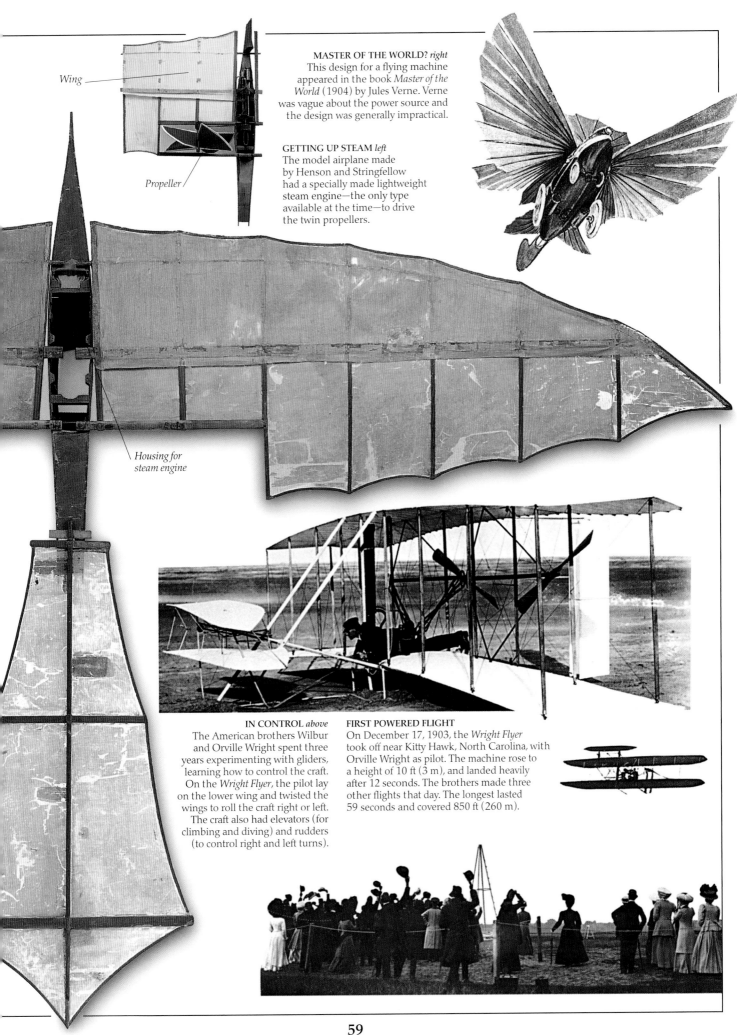

Wing

Propeller

MASTER OF THE WORLD? *right*
This design for a flying machine
appeared in the book *Master of the
World* (1904) by Jules Verne. Verne
was vague about the power source and
the design was generally impractical.

GETTING UP STEAM *left*
The model airplane made
by Henson and Stringfellow
had a specially made lightweight
steam engine—the only type
available at the time—to drive
the twin propellers.

Housing for
steam engine

IN CONTROL *above*
The American brothers Wilbur
and Orville Wright spent three
years experimenting with gliders,
learning how to control the craft.
On the *Wright Flyer*, the pilot lay
on the lower wing and twisted the
wings to roll the craft right or left.
The craft also had elevators (for
climbing and diving) and rudders
(to control right and left turns).

FIRST POWERED FLIGHT
On December 17, 1903, the *Wright Flyer*
took off near Kitty Hawk, North Carolina, with
Orville Wright as pilot. The machine rose to
a height of 10 ft (3 m), and landed heavily
after 12 seconds. The brothers made three
other flights that day. The longest lasted
59 seconds and covered 850 ft (260 m).

Plastics

PLASTICS ARE MATERIALS that can easily be formed into different shapes. They were first used to make imitations of other materials, but it soon became clear that they had useful properties of their own. They are made up of long, chainlike molecules formed by a process (called polymerization) that joins small molecules together. The resulting long molecules give plastics their special properties. The first plastic, Parkesine, was made by modifying cellulose, a chainlike molecule found in most plants. The first truly synthetic plastic was Bakelite, which was invented in 1907. The chemists of the 1920s and 1930s developed ways of making plastics from substances found in oil. Their efforts resulted in a range of materials with different heat, electrical, optical, and molding properties. Plastics such as polyethylene, nylon, and acrylics are widely used today.

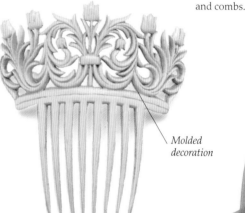

IMITATION IVORY
Early plastics often had the appearance and feel of ivory and carried names such as ivoride. Materials like this were used for knife handles and combs.

Molded decoration

IN FLAMES
In the 1860s, a plastic called celluloid was developed. It was used as a substitute for ivory to make billiard balls and for small items such as this powder box. The new material made little impact at first but, in 1889, George Eastman began using it as a base for photographic film. Unfortunately, it had the disadvantage that it easily caught fire and sometimes exploded.

THE FIRST PLASTIC *right*
In 1856, Alexander Parkes made a hard material that could be molded into shapes. Called Parkesine, it was the first semisynthetic plastic.

Hard, smooth surface

HEAT-PROOF
Leo Baekeland, a Belgium-born chemist working in the US, made a plastic from chemicals found in coal tar. His plastic, which he called Bakelite, was different from earlier plastics because heat made it set hard instead of causing it to melt.

Celluloid box

AROUND THE HOUSE
Plastics of the 1920s and 30s, such as urea formaldehyde, were tough, nontoxic, and could be made any color with synthetic pigments. They were used for boxes, clock cases, piano keys, and lamps.

Heat-proof Bakelite container

Marble-effect surface

Film

Acrylic glasses

Expanded
polystyrene egg
carton

Imitation sponge

Nylon thread

PLASTIC FOAM *above*
Polystyrene was first made in the 1920s. It comes
in two forms: a hard form and a lightweight foam
full of small holes called expanded polystyrene.

NYLON ROPE
Nylon provides
great strength in a
narrow thickness,
making it ideal
for rope.

Molded
polyethylene
shovel and
racket

Buttons
and pen

*Separate
nylon fibers*

Toy blocks

SHAPES AND SIZES
Plastic can be formed into
intricate shapes, such as
this fine netting.

PLASTIC FIBERS *left*
It was American chemist Wallace Carothers who
produced a plastic called nylon in 1934. It was like
artificial silk and could be drawn out into thin threads
and woven into cloth or twined around to create rope as
strong as steel cable. Polyester, another plastic suitable for
fibers, was discovered in 1941. Polyester fibers are woven
into cloth for shirts, pants, and dresses.

Plastic wrench

Polyethylene
flower

The silicon chip

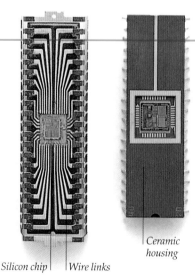

EARLY RADIOS AND TELEVISION SETS used valves (p. 52) to
manipulate their electric currents. These were large, had a
short life, and were costly to produce. In 1947, scientists at
the Bell Telephone Laboratories in the United States invented the
smaller, cheaper, and more reliable transistor to do the same job.
With the development of spacecraft, still smaller components
were needed, and by the end of the 1960s, thousands of
transistors and other electronic components were being
crammed on to chips of silicon only 0.2 in (5 mm) square.
These chips were soon being used to replace the mechanical
control devices in products ranging from dishwashers to cameras.
They were also taking the place
of the bulky electronic circuits in
computers. A computer that took
a whole room to house could
now be contained in a case
that would fit on top of a
desk. A revolution in information
technology followed, with computers
being used for everything from
playing games to administering
government departments.

BABBAGE'S ENGINE
The ancestor of the
computer was Charles
Babbage's "Difference
Engine," a mechanical
calculating device
developed from the 1820s
until the 1840s. Today, tiny
chips do the job of such
cumbersome mechanisms.

*Silicon wafer
containing
several hundred
tiny chips*

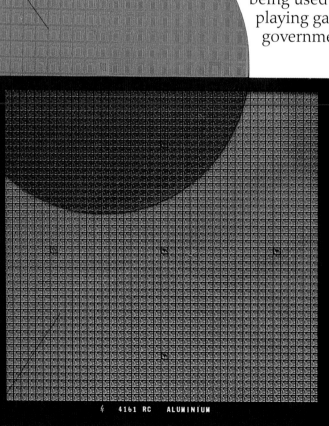

*Matrix of
connections
to be produced*

4161 RC   ALUMINIUM

Silicon chip   *Wire links*

*Ceramic
housing*

SILICON CRYSTAL
Silicon is usually found combined with
oxygen as silica, one form of which is
quartz. Pure silicon is dark gray, hard,
nonmetallic, and forms crystals.

MAKING A CHIP
The electrical components and connections are built up in layers
on a wafer of pure silicon 0.02 in (0.5 mm) thick. First, chemical
impurities are embedded in specific regions of the silicon to
alter their electrical properties. Then aluminum connections
(the equivalent of conventional wires) are laid on top.

CHIP OFF THE OLD BLOCK
In the early 1970s, different types
of chip were developed to do specific
jobs—such as memory chips and
central processing chips. Each silicon
chip, a few millimeters square, is
mounted in a frame of connections
and pins, made of copper coated
with gold or tin. Fine gold wires link
connector pads around the edge
of the chip to the frame. The whole
assembly is housed in a protective
insulating block.

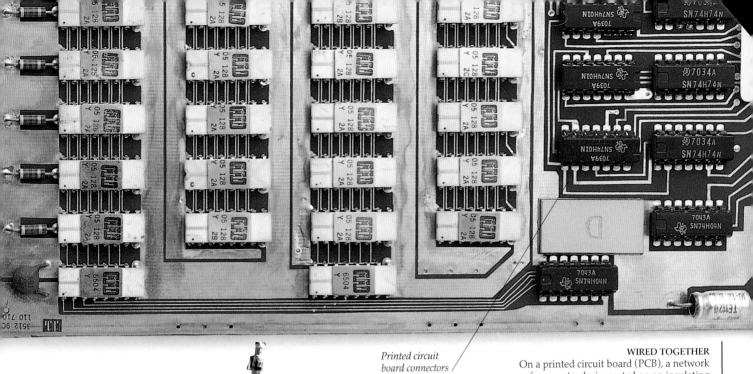

Printed circuit board connectors

WIRED TOGETHER
On a printed circuit board (PCB), a network of copper tracks is created on an insulating board. Components, including silicon chips, are plugged or soldered into holes in the PCB.

OUT IN SPACE
Computers are essential for spacecraft like this satellite. The silicon chip means that control devices can be housed in the limited space on board.

Visual display unit (VDU)

DESKTOP BRAIN
Small modern computers first appeared in the late 1970s. In the US, Commodore introduced the PET, one of the first mass-produced personal computers. It was used mainly in businesses and schools.

Keyboard

ON THE RIGHT TRACK
Under a microscope, the circuitry of a chip looks like a network of aluminum tracks and islands of silicon treated to conduct electricity.

Silicon chip

TOUCH TECHNOLOGY
Tablet computers, also known as tablets, are small computers that are contained in single panels. These tablets have touchscreens, which means they can be operated by touching areas on the screen. The iPad, first launched in 2010, is one of the most successful tablets.

SMART PHONE CARD
Smart cards contain a microprocessor and memory on a single silicon chip. When this card is inserted into a phone, the chip receives power and data through the gold contacts. It can then do security checks and record how many units have been used.

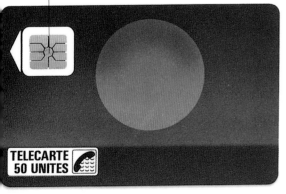

TELECARTE 50 UNITES

Touchscreen

Did you know?

AMATING FACTS

TetraPak milk carton

The TetraPak carton was launched in 1952 by Swedish businessman Ruben Rausing. Its clever design is ideal for holding liquids such as milk, juice, and soup.

Bar codes were first introduced in 1974. A laser scanner "reads" the bar-coded number so that a computer can look up information such as name and price.

Modern snowmobile

The first hovercraft, *SR.N1*, was launched in 1959. It was designed by a British engineer, Christopher Cockerell. The craft glided across water or land, supported on a cushion of air that was contained by a rubberized skirt.

The first graphical computer game was *Spacewar!*. It was developed in 1962 by a college student at the Massachusetts Institute of Technology (MIT).

In 2001, Robert Tools received the first self-contained artificial heart. The grapefruit-sized AbioCor runs on a battery implanted in the rib cage. Earlier artificial hearts needed an outside power source, so anyone who received one had wires sticking out of his or her chest.

The Chinese invented the first toothbrushes about 500 years ago. They were made from pigs' bristles. The first nylon brushes were made in the 1930s.

The Poma® wearable computer

Wearable computers for the consumer market were unveiled in 2002, when the American company Xybernaut® showed off Poma® to the world. "Poma®" is short for "portable multimedia appliance." The central processing unit clips on to the user's belt, while a 1-in- (2.5-cm-) square monitor sits in front of one eye.

Global positioning system (GPS) receivers were developed for the US Air Force in the 1970s. By cross-referencing information from several satellites, a receiver can work out its precise location.

The Aqua-Lung was invented in 1943 by French engineer Emile Gagnan and oceanographer Jacques Cousteau, who also developed an improved method of filming underwater. Cousteau used his inventions to show television viewers the wonders of the undersea world.

Diver and inventor Jacques Cousteau

The modern snowmobile was created in the 1950s by Canadian inventor Joseph-Armand Bombardier. A little like a motorcycle on skis, it is used in snowy regions by forest workers, rescue workers, and the police. It is also popular as a leisure and racing vehicle.

Some of the equipment that John Logie Baird used to build his first television system included a bicycle light and a knitting needle!

The computer mouse was invented in 1965 by Doug Engelbart. It was not called a mouse, though. He called it an "X-Y position indicator."

The first compact discs (CDs) went on sale in 1982. Originally meant to store music, they were also used for photos and computer programs. Later, they evolved into DVDs that can hold about seven times more data and are widely used to store movies.

An ancient Greek designed the world's first vending machine. Around 60 CE, Hero of Alexandria came up with a drink dispenser. Putting a coin in the slot opened a valve that released holy water.

Teflon, the nonstick plastic pan coating, was found by accident. Chemist Roy Plunkett discovered it in 1938, while testing the gas tetrafluoroethylene. Teflon is able to withstand temperatures as low as −450°F (−270°C) and as high as 480°F (250°C).

Bubble gum was invented in 1928 by Walter Diemer. He adapted an existing recipe for chewing gum so that it could be used to blow bubbles.

QUESTIONS AND ANSWERS

Dean Kamen on his Segway HT

Q Are there any famous contemporary inventors?

A It seems as if the past is full of famous inventors but, in the modern world, products are usually created by teams of people working for large companies. Dean L. Kamen is one of the few famous names in the world of inventing. While still a student, Kamen designed a wearable infusion pump that injects sick patients with exact doses of the drugs they need. Next, he developed portable insulin pumps and kidney dialysis machines. Not all of Kamen's innovations are in the medical field. In 2001, he unveiled his Segway Human Transporter (HT), a self-balancing transportation device with an integral gyroscope. Kamen envisages that the Segway HT will revolutionize short-distance travel, particularly in cities. Postal workers, for example, will be able to make deliveries far more quickly and efficiently.

Q Which invention shrank the world in three decades?

A The Internet began life in 1963 in the United States as the ARPAnet, a network of computers linked up to protect military data in the event of a nuclear attack. Under ARPAnet there were key advances: email (1971); telnet, a way to control a computer from a distance (1972); and file transfer protocol (FTP), which helps transfer files (1973). By the 1980s, the internet had developed into an international network. But it took until the mid-1990s for the World Wide Web (WWW) technology to improve enough to make the internet a vital tool in universities, businesses, and homes. The web allows people to swap text, sound, still pictures, and movies around the world—in a matter of seconds.

Q Why are most modern inventions created by companies rather than individuals?

A The Japanese electronics company Sony is famous for its groundbreaking inventions including the Walkman, PlayStation, and the AIBO robot dog (the latter produced from 1999 until 2006). Few people could name any of the individuals involved in the creation of these products. With technology becoming more complex, whole teams of specialists are needed to work on different aspects of an invention. Also, building and testing new technologies requires sophisticated, costly machinery that only large corporations can afford. Such companies market new inventions under their own name, a brand that customers will recognize. Even if the product had been invented by an individual employee, the company probably would not market it under the inventor's name. For one thing, at some point in the future, the inventor may go to work for a rival company.

PlayStation 3

Q How do inventors safeguard their best ideas?

A The only way to be sure that no one steals the design of a new invention is to patent it. Each country has its own patent office, where officials register plans, drawings, and specifications. Only an invention that is truly new can be patented. After that, the inventor can sue anyone who tries to make or sell products based on the same idea, unless they have paid for permission to use it.

Q Could inventions ever outwit inventors?

A At the moment, even the most powerful "supercomputers" have less than half the brainpower of a mouse. These would be capable of testing ideas through trial and error, thereby learning from their mistakes. Currently, the most advanced machines have the mental capacity of a mouse, but designs are always improving.

Record Breakers

⏳ **FASTEST LAND VEHICLE**
A jet-powered car called *ThrustSSC* set the one-mile land speed record in Nevada in 1997, running at 763 mph (1,228 km/h). The car was designed by British engineer John Ackroyd.

⏳ **FASTEST TRANSISTOR**
The world's fastest transistors (computer memory switches) can turn on and off hundreds of billions of times a second. Some of their computers are just 10 nanometers long— $1/8000$ of the width of a human hair.

⏳ **MOST PATENTS**
American inventor Thomas Edison filed 1,093 patents during his lifetime. They included 141 patents for batteries and 389 for electric light and power.

⏳ **BIGGEST RADIO TELESCOPE**
The biggest single-dish radio telescope is 1,000 ft (305 m) across. However, the Very Large Array (VLA) in New Mexico is even more powerful. It is made up of 27 dishes working together as a single telescope.

Inside an Internet cafe

Timeline of inventions

Silicon wafer, 1981

THE HISTORY OF INVENTION begins when our earliest ancestors started to use tools, more than three million years ago. Since then, humankind has continued to employ intelligence and resourcefulness to make useful technologies that help change our world. Any timeline of invention must omit far more than it includes. Here are just a few important tools, instruments, and machines that have been invented over the last 10,000 years.

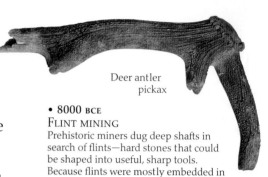

Deer antler pickax

• 8000 BCE
FLINT MINING
Prehistoric miners dug deep shafts in search of flints—hard stones that could be shaped into useful, sharp tools. Because flints were mostly embedded in soft chalk, the miners used deer antlers as simple picks.

8000 BCE

• 100 BCE
SCREW PRESS
The screw press was invented by the Greeks. They would place grapes, olives, or even clothes between the two boards. They turned the screw to press the top board down hard, squeezing out the juice, oil, or excess water.

Screw press

• 550 CE
ASTROLABE
The astrolabe was an instrument that enabled travelers to find their latitude by studying the position of the stars. It was first invented by Arab astronomers.

Astrolabe

• 1088 CE
MECHANICAL CLOCK
The first mechanical clock was a complicated tower of wheels and gears, invented by Su Sung. It used a waterwheel that moved the mechanism forward every time one of its buckets filled up. Every 24 hours, a metal globe representing the Earth turned on its axis once.

Su Sung's mechanical clock tower

100 BCE　　　　**550 CE**　　　　**1088 CE**

• 1892 CE
VISCOSE RAYON
This artificial fiber was the first realistic alternative to silk. Three British chemists discovered the process for making it, starting out with a natural ingredient, cellulose, found in cotton and wood pulp.

Rayon fabric

• 1948 CE
POLAROID CAMERA
The first "instant" camera was the Polaroid Land camera, invented by American Edwin Land. The camera used special film that contained the necessary developing chemicals. One minute after taking the picture, a brown and white photograph came out.

Classic Polaroid camera

• 1965 CE
COMPUTER MOUSE
The mouse was invented by US engineer Doug Engelbart in 1965. The first personal computer to use it was the Apple Mac, launched in 1984. Until then, people had to use keyboard commands.

Computer mouse

1892 CE　　　　**1948 CE**　　　　**1965 CE**

Roman scales

• 4000 BCE
SCALES
The Sumerians invented the beam balance, where a measuring pan is hung from each end of a wooden or metal beam. Later peoples, including the Romans, improved on this basic principle.

Chinese writing

• 1500 BCE
CHINESE WRITING
Chinese is the oldest surviving written language. Like the first written language, Sumerian cuneiform, Chinese characters started out as pictograms—pictures of objects and ideas—that were gradually stylized.

• 600 BCE
ARCHIMEDEAN SCREW
This device is named after the Greek thinker Archimedes, who described one he saw being used in Egypt around 260 BCE. The screw is a pump. It pushes water up along the "thread" of the cylinder as the user turns the screw.

Archimedean screw

| 4000 BCE | 1500 BCE | 600 BCE |

• 1643 CE
BAROMETER
The barometer, an instrument that measures air pressure, was invented by Italian physicist Evangelista Torricelli. He put a dish over the end of a closed tube of mercury, then inverted both of them. The mercury fell until its level balanced the pressure of the air.

Torricelli's barometer

• 1788 CE
THRESHING MACHINE
Threshing means separating grains of corn from the husk, or chaff. It used to be done by beating harvested corn with a stick, but in 1788 Scottish millwright Andrew Meikle invented a machine to do the job.

Threshing machine

Leclanché cell

• 1866 CE
LECLANCHÉ CELL
French engineer Georges Leclanché created the forerunner of the modern battery. The negative terminal was a jar with a zinc rod in an ammonium chloride solution. Inside this was the positive terminal, a smaller pot with a carbon rod in manganese dioxide.

| 1643 CE | 1788 CE | 1866 CE |

• 1983 CE
DYSON CYCLONIC CLEANER
British inventor James Dyson came up with the first bagless vacuum cleaner. His inspiration was an industrial cyclone, a whirling device used by factories to suck dust particles from air. Dyson made his first model of a bagless cleaner in 1978. His G-Force cyclonic cleaner went on sale in Japan eight years later.

Dyson multi-cyclone cleaner

• 2002 CE
ROOMBA ROBOT VACUUM CLEANER
These battery powered cleaners automatically detect dirt and avoid obstacles, while sensors prevent them from falling off edges (such as down a stair).

Roomba vacuum cleaner

• 2007 CE
iPHONE
A smartphone is a cell phone that can do similar things to a computer, including sending emails and browsing websites. The Apple company introduced the first smartphone, called the iPhone, in 2007. Smartphones have large touchscreens that are easy to use and can display different kinds of information in different ways.

iPhone

| 1983 CE | 2002 CE | 2007 CE |

Find out more

IF YOU ARE INTERESTED in inventions, you will soon notice that you come across hundreds of them every day—and many of them are in your own home. Visits to science museums can give lots of helpful information about inventions, including hands-on demonstrations of how they work. Look for useful books, websites, and television programs, too. Best of all, see if you can come up with some inventions of your own. Start with sketches and descriptions, then build up to making a working model. Good luck!

The food mixer is one of many inventions that can be found in the average home

OLD VALVE RADIO
All inventors learn valuable lessons by looking at the inventions of the past. Shop flea markets for cheap old radios or other machines. Compare your finds to their modern versions. How have radios changed since this one was made? What features have disappeared? Which are still there? And what can modern radios do that this one cannot?

USEFUL WEBSITES

- A website with a timeline, plus A–Zs of inventors and inventions: **inventors.about.com**
- Lots of explanations of scientific principles and inventions: **www.howstuffworks.com**
- A website from MIT about inventors and inventions: **http://web.mit.edu/invent/**
- Website for the Tech Museum of Innovation, California: **www.thetech.org**

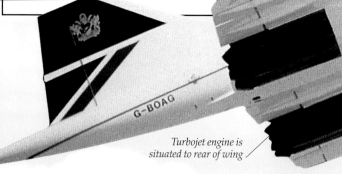

Turbojet engine is situated to rear of wing

THE CONCORDE, AN INVENTION OF THE SKIES
Fly away on vacation, or simply look up to see some of humankind's most amazing inventions—aircraft. Jet passenger planes have been around since 1952, while the first supersonic craft, the *Concorde*, made its maiden flight in 1969. Flying at twice the speed of sound, the *Concorde* cut the time of a transatlantic flight to three hours, 20 minutes. Only 14 of the planes entered service, and the final flight was made in 2003.

THE SCIENCE MUSEUM
A key attraction at London's Science Museum is the Making the Modern World gallery. It displays 150 milestone inventions created from 1750 to 2000. Highlights include the *Apollo 10* Command Module, used in the first Moon landing.

GEODESIC DOME
This eye-catching building is La Géode, an OMNIMAX movie theater where visitors can enjoy the latest cinematic technologies, including a 360° movie screen. It is in the Parc de la Villette, Paris. If you cannot get to Paris, see if there is an OMNIMAX or IMAX theater near you. The quality of the picture and sound make for quite an experience.

SMART WASHING MACHINE
Familiar appliances are being improved all the time. The latest "smart" kitchen machines are Internet linked so that owners can control them remotely by email. This washing machine will even call out a service technician if it breaks down.

Rotating drum spins washing

Optical viewfinder

AMERA CURIOUS
ind out more about a popular nvention, such as the camera. ompare a digital camera with an old odel. Digital cameras do not use film. nstead, they have a sensor that converts light photons) into electrical charges (electrons). ou can also read about the development photography in specialized magazines.

Places to visit

THE EXPLORATORIUM, SAN FRANCISCO, CALIFORNIA
Hundreds of fun and innovative exhibits demonstrate scientific principles.

SCIENCE MUSEUM OF MINNESOTA, ST. PAUL, MINNESOTA
Visitors can try experiments exploring physical science and mathematics.

FORT LAUDERDALE MUSEUM OF DISCOVERY AND SCIENCE, FORT LAUDERDALE, FLORIDA
Lets visitors discover the universal concepts behind today's technology.

BRADBURY SCIENCE MUSEUM, LOS ALAMOS, NEW MEXICO
Home to exhibits about the history of Los Alamos National Laboratory and its research.

BRITISH AIRWAYS

Distinctive, pointed nose cuts through the air

Wings form streamlined "V" shape

Passengers safe in pressurized cabin

ROBOT WARS
Computer scientists are trying to make robots more intelligent by getting them to compete against each other. Since 1999, robot teams have been competing in the RoboCup soccer tournament. Mostly the teams are made up of identical robots. Even though the robots are only about 12 in (30 cm) tall and move slowly, it is still exciting to see them mimic human behavior.

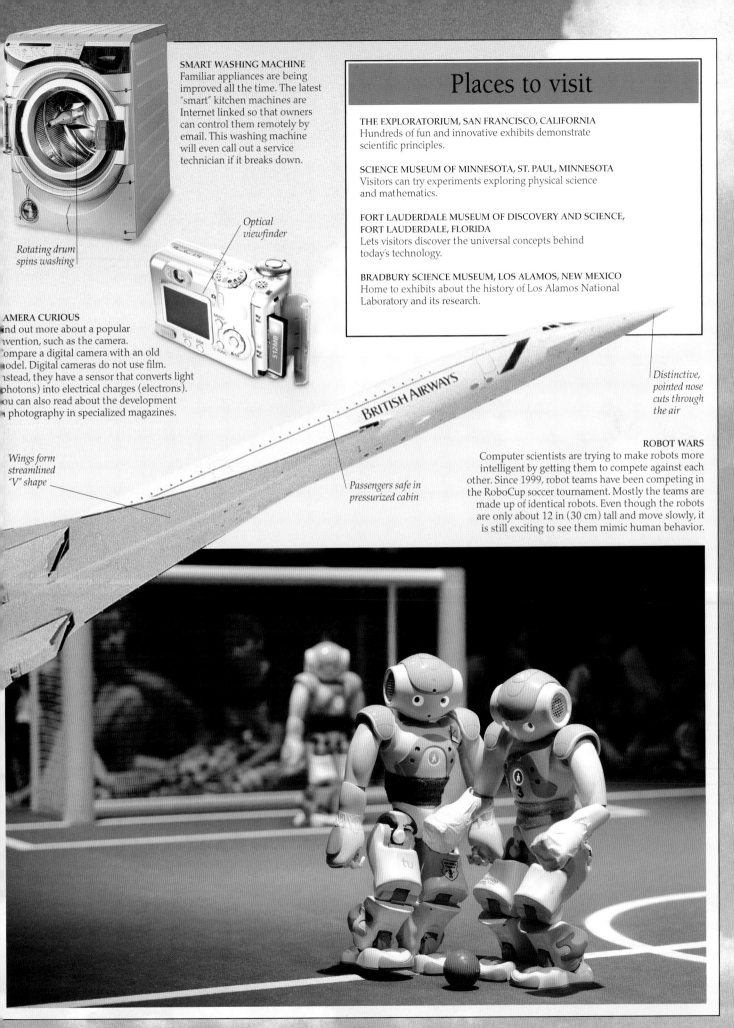

Glossary

Flint
(used as a
simple ax)

AMPUTATION A type of surgery in which a limb, such as the leg, is removed. It is less common now that medical innovations have made it possible to cure many infections and injuries.

ANESTHETIC A substance used to block pain signals from the body to the brain. In medical operations, the anesthetic effect may be local to the part of the body being operated on, or it may be general, affecting the whole body.

ANGLE Two straight lines leaving a single point make a corner that can be described by its angle—the portion they would make of any circle centered on the point. Circles are given 360°, so the two hands of a clock at 3 p.m., which take a quarter of the circle, form an angle of 90°.

ANODE A positive electrode, taken to be the source of current flowing into its surroundings. (see also **ELECTRODE**)

AUTOMATIC Any system or machine that works by itself without external control or effort by a person.

BEAM In machines and buildings, a strong horizontal supporting bar made of wood or metal that carries forces across distances.

CALCULATE In mathematics, to figure out the answer according to a rule-governed method. The word comes from the pebbles that were used in the Roman era to help with math problems; they were called calx.

CATHODE A negative electrode that receives current from its surroundings. The flow of electricity into a cathode can be used to coat an object in silver—the object is wired up as a cathode and attracts tiny particles of silver. (see also **ELECTRODE**)

COMPOUND A chemical substance formed when two or more other substances combine with each other.

CULTIVATE To work toward the best possible growth of plants, especially by plowing, fertilizing, and weeding fields, and by rotating crops to maintain the balance of nutrients in the soil.

CYLINDER In engines, the tubular chamber in which the pressure is created to push the other parts. In gasoline engines, the larger the cylinder (measured in liters), the more power the engine can create.

DIAPHRAGM A thin, strong sheet of material, often circular, designed to flex in the middle. A large diaphragm divides the human body between the chest and the stomach to aid breathing.

EFFICIENT Describes a machine or system that does a job with very little wasted energy or human effort.

ELECTRICAL Describes any thing or event in which electricity has a significant role.

ELECTRICITY Energy associated with electrically charged particles, usually electrons, either when they are moving, as in a wire, or stationary, as in a battery.

ELECTRODE The source or destination of an electric current in a cell such as a battery. Electrodes can be made from a range of materials, often metallic.

EXPERIMENT A controlled test of a theory, or part of a theory, used to provide evidence for or against a scientific idea.

FLINT A common type of stone, with the useful property of breaking and chipping in a way that produces sharp edges. Flint was widely mined in prehistoric times and used to make simple tools.

FOCUS The point where rays of light meet after passing through a lens.

Giant pulleys in an elevator

FORCE A push or pull that can make something move, prevent it from moving, or change its motion.

FRICTION The resistance to movement between two surfaces in contact. This force can generate heat, as when rubbing your hands together for warmth.

GEAR A wheel with teeth that carries power from one moving part to another. On a bicycle, gears are used to allow efficient cycling at different speeds. Closely related to gears are pulleys, which have no teeth and are used with ropes. They are used in elevators and in construction to lift heavy loads.

Chopsticks use a system of leverage

GENERATOR A machine using the motion of a wire coil past magnets to turn movement into electricity—the opposite of an electric motor. A bicycle dynamo is a simple example.

INDUSTRIAL REVOLUTION The dramatic change from a farming society to a mechanized society, first identified in the UK toward the end of the 1700s. Important parts of the process include the relocation of large numbers of people from the countryside to towns, and the introduction of powered machines in most aspects of industry.

INFORMATION TECHNOLOGY Machines, programs, and systems designed to help process information, often more efficiently and reliably than humans can. The best example is computers.

IRRIGATION Systems of dams, canals, pipes, and other tools that help us to maintain a steady water supply to crops, especially in areas with unpredictable rainfall.

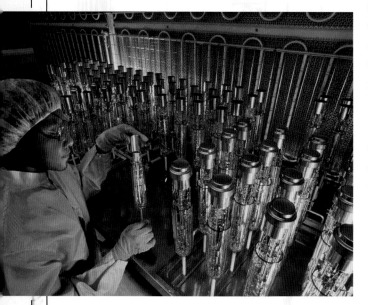

Making cathode ray tubes in a factory

Helicopter with its rotary blades in motion

LOGARITHM A way to represent numbers as powers of another number, such as 10. The "log" of 100 is 2, because $100 = 10^2$. Logs can represent only positive numbers. Adding logs is equivalent to multiplying the numbers they represent. First slide rules and then calculators have made this process automatic.

MECHANICAL A device or process that uses moving parts (such as levers or wheels) instead of electricity or electronics.

MEDIUM The material or system a signal or energy passes through from one point to another.

MOLECULE The basic unit of a chemical compound, consisting of two or more atoms bonded together. Molecules vary in size. Extremely long molecules are used to make some modern materials, such as plastic wrap.

PHENOMENON An experience or event, particularly as it is sensed by a human observer.

PISTON A flat-headed tubular machine part that moves up and down within a cylinder. A piston may be mechanically driven to pump gases or fluids in the chamber or may transfer pressure in the cylinder to drive other parts of the machine.

PIVOT A machine part around which another machine part moves. Pivots may be simple hinges or more complicated structures. They are also known as bearings, since they normally "bear" a load.

PRESSURE The "pressing" force of one substance against another. Usually applies to flexible materials, such as liquids or gases, for example, the air inside a car tire.

LEVER A rigid bar pivoted at one point along its length and used to transmit force. If the distant end of the lever travels farther than the load (near the pivot point), the lever "magnifies" the force that can be applied.

LIFT The force required to overcome the weight of a flying machine and keep it off the ground. In an airplane, lift is created by passing air over the curved, angled wings. The fast-flowing air pushes against their lower surface and forces the plane up.

PRISM A transparent object, normally glass, used to change the direction of a beam of light. Prisms are often used to split light into separate beams.

RECEIVER The instrument that detects and translates a signal into a form—such as sound waves—that humans can sense. An everyday example is the radio or "tuner" component in a music system.

RESERVOIR A container for storing liquids, such as machine oil or drinking water.

SEAL A tight join, often using rubber or another waterproof material that prevents gas or liquid from escaping or entering an enclosed space.

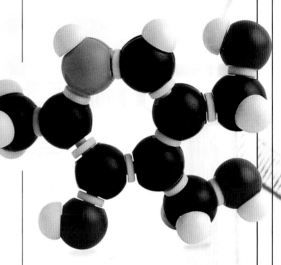

Colored balls represent the arrangement of atoms in a molecule of vitamin B6

SOLUTION In liquids, a solution is a mixture of one liquid with something else—another liquid, a gas, or a solid.

TECHNOLOGY The practical uses of knowledge—in terms of skills, and the creation and use of new tools. New technology is driven both by new scientific discoveries and new uses for old knowledge.

TRANSMITTER An instrument that translates a signal into a form in which it can be passed through a particular medium to a receiver. Examples include a cell phone or walkie-talkie.

VACUUM A perfectly empty—or very nearly empty—space. A vacuum can be created in a vessel by pumping out all the gases or liquids inside.

VALVE A flap or plug used to control the flow of gas or liquid from one space to another. Some valves control the direction of flow, some the timing of the flow. Valves are vital for most pumping systems. Their existence in human arteries led scientists to discover the heart's true function—a pump.

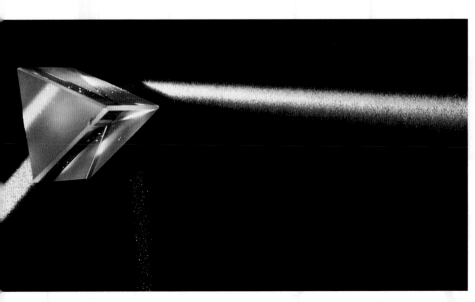

This prism is splitting white light into separate beams, revealing a rainbow of colors

Index

Acknowledgments

Dorling Kindersley would like to thank:
The following members of the staff of the Science Museum, London, for help with the provision of objects for photography and checking the text: Marcus Austin, Peter Bailes, Brian Bowers, Roger Bridgman, Neil Brown, Jane Bywaters, Sue Cackett, Janet Carding, Ann Carter, Jon Darius, Eryl Davies, Sam Evans, Peter Fitzgerald, Jane Insley, Stephen Johnston, Ghislaine Lawrence, Peter Mann, Mick Marr, Kate Morris, Susan Mossman, Andrew Nahum, Cathy Needham, Francesca Riccini, Derek Robinson, Peter Stephens, Frazer Swift, Peter Tomlinson, John Underwood, Denys Vaughan, Tony Vincent, John Ward, Anthony Wilson, David Woodcock, Michael Wright.
Retouching: Roy Flooks **Index:** Helen Peters
Proofreading: Monica Byles

Picture credits
t=top, b=bottom, m=middle, l=left, r=right
Alamy Images: Judith Collins 65tc, Neil Fraser 63br, Interfoto 58cr, Oleksiy Maksymenko Photography 67bc, sciencephotos 39bl; Ann Ronan Picture Library: 17tl, 29cr, 29bm, 35br,

38tl, 38mr, 44tl, 44tr, 45tl, 56br; Bridgeman Art Library: 11,18bm, 19bl; /Russian Museum, Leningrad 21 mr, 22tr; /Giraudon /Musée des Beaux Arts, Vincennes 30bl, 50mr; British Airways: 68–69m; Corbis: James Blank 25tc, Zero Creatives / cultura 24tl, Peter Ginter/ Science Faction 64–65 (background), 66–67 (background), Imaginechina 65br, Haruyoshi Yamaguchi/Sygma 65tr; Brian Cosgrove Collection: 68–69; Design Museum: 68tl; E.T. Archive: 26tr; Dreamstime.com: Chris Dorney 61tc; Vivien Fifield: 32m, 48ml, 48m, 48bl; Getty Images: Gabriel Bouys/AFP 67br, Imagno/Hulton Archive 58b, Patrik Stollarz/AFP 69b, Bruce Forster 70bl; Michael Holford: 16ml, 18ml, 18bl; Hulton-Deutsch: 41tr; Barnabas Kindersley: 64ml; Mary Evans Picture Library: 10m, 12ml, 12tr, 14, 19mr, 19br, 20tr, 21mr, 23tr, 24tr, 25tr, 28br, 30br, 31mr, 39m, 40tl, 40mr, 41tm, 42bl, 42ml, 43tr, 43m, 50br, 53mr, 54tl, 54bl, 55ml; Mentorn Barraclough Carey Productions Ltd: 69br Copyright © 2002 Robot Wars LLC/ Robot Wars Ltd. Trademarks: Robot Wars and the Robot Wars logo are trademarks of Robot Wars LLC. Sir Killalot, Shunt, Matilda, Sgt Bash,

Dead Metal, Mr Psycho, Growler and Refbot are trademarks and designs of the BBC in the UK and are used under licence. Sir Killalot, Shunt, Matilda, Sgt Bash, Dead Metal, Mr Psycho, Growler and Refbot are trademarks of Robot Wars LLC in the world excluding the UK. The Robot Wars television series is produced by Mentorn in association with Robot Wars Ltd for BBC Television in the UK and for broadcasters worldwide; National Maritime Museum, London: 64–65; National Motor Museum, Beaulieu: 49tr; Natural History Museum, London: 66tr; Norfolk Rural Life Museum: 67mr; Stephen Oliver: 67bl, 68br; Popperfoto: 64b; Rex Features: 69tl; / Patrick Barth 65b; /Erik C. Pendzich 65tl; Science Museum, London: 66br, 70tl, 71b; Science & Society Picture Library: 63m, 63bl, 63bm, 67ml, 67m; Syndication International: 12tl, 13m, 23tl, 26mr, 28tl, 28mr, 34tl, 35tl, 36tr, 46br, 50br, 52b, 52tr, 56tr, 58bm, 59br; /Bayerische Staatsbibliotek, Munich 24cl; /British Museum 13tm, 24bl, 59tr; /Library of Congress 37tl; / Smithsonian Institution, Washington DC 58br; Wallace Collection: 66ml; Photo Courtesy of Xybernaut Corporation: 64tr

Jacket images: *Front:* Alamy Images: BananaStock b; Dorling Kindersley: Design Museum, London tr, The Science Museum, London tl, tl/ (Axe), tc; *Back:* Dorling Kindersley: The Science Museum, London tr, cb, crb, cl, bl, bc

Wallchart: Alamy Images: Neil Fraser br; Corbis: Library of Congress - digital ve/Science Faction cb/ (Airplane); Dorling Kindersley: Pitt Rivers Museum, University of Oxford tl, tl/ (Bow Drill), tl/(Wooden Hearth), The Science Museum, London cla, cl, c, tr, cra, cr, clb, cb, cr/ (Stethoscope), clb/(Reeds and rushes), bl, bl/ (Voltaic pile), fcr

With the exception of the items listed above, and the objects on pages 8–9, 61, and 64–71, all the photographs in this book are of objects in the collections of the Science Museum, London

All other images © Dorling Kindersley
For further information see: www.dkimages.com